TALENT SEARCH TESTS

FOR SCHOOL CHILDREN
5TH, 6TH & 7TH STDs.

By
V.V.K. Subburaj

YOUNG KIDS PRESS
An imprint of Sura Books (Pvt) Ltd.
(An ISO 9001:2000 Certified Company)
Chennai ● Ernakulam
Bengalooru ● Thiruvananthapuram

Price: Rs.80.00

© PUBLISHERS

TALENT SEARCH FOR SCHOOL CHILDREN (5TH, 6TH & 7TH STDS.)

By
V.V.K. Subburaj

THIS EDITION : FEBRUARY, 2009
SIZE : 1/4 CROWN
PAGES : 112

Price: Rs.80.00
ISBN: 81-7254-277-1

YOUNG KIDS PRESS
[An imprint of Sura Books (Pvt) Ltd.]

Head Office : 1620, 'J' Block, 16th Main Road, Anna Nagar, **Chennai - 600 040.** Phones: 044-26162173, 26161099.

Branches :
- XXXII/2328, New Kalavath Road, Opp. to BSNL, Near Chennoth Glass, Palarivattom, **Ernakulam - 682 025.** Phones: 0484-3205797, 2535636
- TC 27/2162, Chirakulam Road, Statue, **Thiruvananthapuram - 695 001.** Phone : 0471-2570445.
- 3638/A, IVth Cross, Opp. to Malleswaram Railway Station, Gayathri Nagar, Back gate of Subramaniya Nagar, **Bengalooru - 560 021.** Phone: 080-23324950

Printed at T. Krishna Press, Chennai - 600 102 and Published by V.V.K.Subburaj for Young Kids Press [An imprint of Sura Books (Pvt) Ltd.] 1620, 'J' Block, 16th Main Road, Anna Nagar, Chennai - 600 040. Phones: 26162173, 26161099. Fax: (91) 44-26162173. e-mail: enquiry@surabooks.com; website: www.surabooks.com

○ TEST No.1 ○

General Knowledge

1. Seismograph is an instrument to measure
   a) Earthquake shocks b) Air pressure
   c) Air temperature d) Height

2. The name of the first man to reach the North Pole is
   a) Armstrong b) Robert Peary
   c) Tenzing d) Hillary

3. What did Madam Curie discover?
   a) Radioactivity b) Wireless
   c) Aeroplane d) Radium

4. The discoverer of Raman Effect was
   a) C.V. Raman b) Newton
   c) Jagdish Chandra Bose
   d) Einstein

5. 'The Lion of Punjab' is the name given to
   a) Bal Gangadhar Tilak
   b) Lala Lajpat Rai
   c) Mohammad Ali Jinnah
   d) Seth Govind Das

6. By which term Sarojini Naidu was called
   a) A worker of the Congress
   b) A poetess
   c) Nightingale of India
   d) Famous leader

7. Kolkata is known as
   a) City of Palaces b) Port
   c) Trade centre d) Megalopolis

8. Which country is known as the 'Land of Midnight Sun?'
   a) Sweden b) Denmark
   c) Lapland d) Norway

9. The first general elections in India were held in
   a) 1947 b) 1950
   c) 1951 d) 1952

10. The last Governor-General of India was
    a) Lord Mountbatten
    b) C. Rajagopalachari
    c) Rajendra Prasad
    d) Mahatma Gandhi

11. Who is the Supreme Commander of all the forces in India?
    a) Army Commander
    b) Commander of Air Force
    c) Prime Minister of India
    d) President of India

12. The grandfather of Akbar was
    a) Aurangzeb b) Shah Alam
    c) Babur d) Humayun

13. The President of Bharatiya Janata Party is
    a) Venkaiah Naidu b) Bal Thakre
    c) Ashok Singhal d) Rajnath Singh

14. Ban-Ki-moon is
    a) A Chairman of International Monetary Fund
    b) A Secretary-General of United Nations Organisation
    c) A President of Angola
    d) A noted scientist

15. President of Iraq is
    a) Saddam Hussain b) Nawaz Sharif
    c) Yasser Arafat d) Jalal Talabani

16. The Finance Minister of India is
    a) Kumara Mangalam
    b) Jaswant Singh
    c) P. Chidambaram
    d) Pranab Mukherjee

17. The city, near which Sarnath temple is located is
    a) Sanchi b) Gaya
    c) Lumbini d) Varanasi

18. India has
    a) 15 states b) 21 states
    c) 28 states d) 26 states

19. The state with the largest population in India is
    a) Uttar Pradesh b) Andra Pradesh
    c) Madhya Pradesh d) Maharashtra

20. The largest State in area is
    a) Uttar Pradesh b) Rajasthan
    c) Maharashtra d) Andra Pradesh

21. The President of India must have completed the age of
    a) 25 years   b) 35 years
    c) 30 years   d) 40 years

22. The salary of the President of India per month is
    a) Rs.1,50,000   b) Rs.1,10,000
    c) Rs.1,25,000   d) Rs.80,000

23. The term of the President of India is
    a) 3 years   b) 4 years
    c) 5 years   d) 7 years

24. All Ministers at the centre are appointed by
    a) The Prime Minister
    b) The President
    c) The Vice-President
    d) Home Minister

25. The Lok Sabha has a life of
    a) 5 years
    b) 8 years
    c) 7 years
    d) 6 years

Reasoning - General Intelligence

Directions (Qns. 1-5): In each question, there is a relationship between two terms to the left of : :, the same relationship is there between the two terms on the right of :: One term is missing. Find out the same from the given alternatives.

1. AGM : CGK : : CIO : ?
    a) EJM   b) EIO
    c) EGM   d) EIM

2. BGL : AEN : : DJF : ?
    a) EFI   b) CHH
    c) EFB   d) FIA

3. ADGJ : ? : : EHKN : VSPN
    a) QTWZ   b) ZWTQ
    c) TQWZ   d) TQZW

4. BGL : VQL : : DIN : ?
    a) XTN   b) XSM
    c) XSN   d) YSN

5. AFK : OJE :: HMR : ?
    a) VQL   b) VQM
    c) WQL   d) VRM

Directions (Qns. 6-10): In these questions, old signs have been given new ones, as below:

V stands for +
^ stands for –
N stands for ×
X stands for ÷
M stands for =

Which relationship is true in each case? Find out the correct alternatives.

6. a) 24 V 6 X 1 M 30
    b) 24 ^ 6 X 1 M 30

c) 24 X 6 ^ 1 M 30
d) 24 ^ 6 N 1 M 30

7. a) 24 6 M 4 N 6
    b) 24 V 6 M 5 N 6
    c) 24 X 6 M 4 V 6
    d) 24 M 6 V 4 ^ 6

8. a) 25 ^ V 2 ^ 10 M 40
    b) 25 X 2 V 10 M 40
    c) 25 2 V 10 M 40
    d) 25 N 2 ^ 10 M 40

9. a) 5 ^ M 6 V 5 N 40 ^ 5
    b) 5 N 6 V 5 M 40 ^ 5
    c) 5 ^ 6 V 5 N 40 M 5
    d) 5 N 6 ^ 5 M 40 V 5

10. a) 8 V 1 N 7 ^ 3 M 6 N 2
    b) 8 N 1 ^ 7 V 3 M 6 V 2
    c) 8 N 1 V 7 ^ 3 M 6 N 2
    d) 8 X 1 V 7 N 3 M 6 N 2

Directions (Qns. 11 & 12): Observe, the following figures and find out the correct answer to questions.

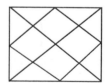

11. How many triangles are there in the above figure?
    a) 20   b) 30
    c) 36   d) 46

12. How many squares are there in the above figure?
    a) 4   b) 5
    c) 6   d) 7

Directions (13-14): *See these pictures, which one is different from others?*

13.

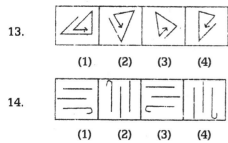

(1)   (2)   (3)   (4)

14.

(1)   (2)   (3)   (4)

15. **What is on the opposite face of A in the cube?**

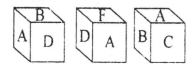

a) B   b) C
c) D   d) E

Directions (16-20): *Each question is based on number series. The number series are based on certain principle. In each question, one number is missing. Identify the correct one from the given alternatives.*

16. 1, 6, 13, 22, 33......., 61
a) 44   b) 45
c) 46   d) 47

17. 7, 9, 12, 14, 17, ...,
a) 19   b) 20
c) 21   d) 22

18. 37, 29, 19, ..., 13, 7
a) 17   b) 16
c) 15   d) 14

19. 0, 7, 26, 63.....
a) 81   b) 99
c) 124   d) 143

20. 1, 8, 9, 64, 25....
a) 132   b) 188
c) 200   d) 216

21. **Add two biggest numbers from 4, 6, 3, 9, 5. Divide it by the smallest number. Then multiply the product with the product number. Now what will be the new number?**
a) 36   b) 25
c) 16   d) 9

22. **A is B's wife and C is A's sister. D is the father of C, while E is D's son. What is the relation of E to B ?**
a) Brother
b) Brother-in-law
c) Cousin
d) Father-in-law

23. **Four persons P, Q, R and S are standing in a row as per their size. Among them P is taller than Q and S is taller than P, but S is smaller than R. Starting from the tallest one, what is the order in the row?**
a) RSPQ   b) PQRS
c) QPRS   d) SRPQ

24. **Hari is older than Hameed but younger than Surendra. Harpreet is younger than Hareendra but older than Hameed. Mahendra is older than Hareendra. Who is the youngest?**
a) Hari   b) Harpreet
c) Surendra   d) Hameed

25. **Ram's sister says to him, "I'll hide myself at a place where you can reach first by going to the north. Then you will have to walk an equal distance to the east. From here you will go twice the distance to the south and finally twice the distance to the west. Which direction, from the place of conversation, is the hiding place?**
a) East   b) West
c) North   d) South West

General English

Directions (1-5): *Choose the word which is opposite in meaning to the word given in capital.*

1. **WEARY**
a) Tired   b) Haste
c) Waste   d) Jolly

2. **DISPARAGE**
a) Justify   b) Criticise
c) Censure   d) Legally

3. **DISCIPLINE**
a) Order   b) Systematic
c) Indiscipline   d) Standing

4. **BEAUTIFUL**
   a) Good
   b) Attractive
   c) Ugly
   d) Fine

5. **KNOWN**
   a) Gone
   b) Sown
   c) John
   d) Unknown

Directions (6-10): Choose one word for the following utterance from the options given below:

6. **A fire-place where food is cooked**
   a) Hearth
   b) Oven
   c) Gas
   d) Cooking-place

7. **Cat with grey or brownish fur and dark stripes**
   a) Colourful
   b) Multicoloured
   c) Tabby
   d) Brown

8. **Stopped, came to an end**
   a) Over
   b) End
   c) Full-stop
   d) Completed

9. **The changed gender of cock**
   a) Bird
   b) Hen
   c) Peacock
   d) Pigeon

10. **The plural number of fish is**
    a) Fishing
    b) Fish
    c) Black-fish
    d) Fisheries

Directions (11-18): Read the following passage carefully and answer the questions given below:

Whales are the largest animals in the sea. You know that the largest animals on land are elephants. But, compared to a whale, an elephant is a tiny creature. If you put an elephant by the side of a whale, it would look like a cat but for its shape. Whales are huge and heavy giants. The largest whale, the blue whale grows about a hundred feet long. Some of them weigh more than a hundred and twenty tons, while the normal weight of an elephant is not more than seven tons. A whale eats two to three tons of food at a single meal.

11. **Where does the largest animal on earth live?**
    a) Plains
    b) Sea
    c) Mountains
    d) Forests

12. **The largest whale is known as**
    a) Blue whale
    b) Sea whale
    c) Sperm whale
    d) Black whale

13. **The largest animal on land is**
    a) Camel
    b) Giraffe
    c) Elephant
    d) Lion

14. **Compared to a whale, an elephant looks like a**
    a) Giant
    b) Heavy weight animal
    c) Small fry
    d) Cat

15. **The length of a blue whale is about**
    a) 180 feet
    b) 80 feet
    c) 100 feet
    d) 120 feet

16. **Some whales weigh about**
    a) 100 tons
    b) 120 tons
    c) 200 tons
    d) 80 tons

17. **Normal weight of an elephant is**
    a) 7 tons
    b) 8 tons
    c) 6 tons
    d) 9 tons

18. **The amount of food eaten by a whale at a single meal is about**
    a) One to two tons
    b) Two to three tons
    c) Three to four tons
    d) None of the above three weights

Directions (19-25): Fill in the blanks using one of the words given below each sentence.

19. **In the well, water is only 3 metres from the.................**
    a) shallow
    b) surface
    c) dive
    d) bottom

20. **You can................into the well and take the bucket out.**
    a) shallow
    b) surface
    c) dive
    d) bottom

21. **Your heart and lungs .... the cage made for them by your ribs.**
    a) breaths
    b) lungs
    c) occupy
    d) immediately

22. **When you breathe in, your .... fill with air.**
    a) breathe
    b) lungs
    c) occupy
    d) immediately

23. **You ....out immediately after you have breathed in.**
    a) breathe
    b) lungs
    c) occupy
    d) immediately

24. **I searched the ....house.**
    a) alive
    b) single
    c) all
    d) whole

25. **I did not find a single mouse........**
    a) alive
    b) single
    c) all
    d) whole

Arithmetic - Numerical Ability

1. ? × 11 = 55550
    a) 505   b) 5050
    c) 50505   d) 5005

2. ? – 1046 – 398 – 69 = 939
    a) 2502   b) 2512
    c) 2472   d) 1978

3. 1014 × 986 = ?
    a) 998904   b) 999804
    c) 998814   d) 998804

4. ? × 48 = 173 × 240
    a) 545   b) 685
    c) 865   d) 495

5. 42060 ÷ 15 + 5 = ?
    a) 2804   b) 2809
    c) 2103   d) 289

6. LCM of 2/3, 4/9, 5/6 and 7/12 is ?
    a) $\dfrac{1}{18}$ b) $\dfrac{1}{36}$
    c) $\dfrac{35}{9}$ d) $\dfrac{140}{3}$

7. .6 + .66 + .066 + 6.606 = ?
    a) 6.744   b) 6.738
    c) 7.932   d) 7.388

8. 0.001 ÷ ? = 0.01
    a) 10   b) .1
    c) .01   d) .001

9. .24 × .35   = ?   .14 × .15 × .02
    a) 2   b) 20
    c) 200   d) 2000

10. What decimal of an hour is a second?
    a) .0025   b) .0256
    c) .00027   d) .000126

11. If 12276 ÷ 155 = 79.2, the value of 122.76 ÷ 15.5 is ?
    a) 7.092   b) 7.92
    c) 79.02   d) 79.2

12. $\dfrac{35 \times 0.0015}{0.25 \times 0.07} =$
    a) 0.3   b) 3
    c) 30   d) 4

13. 9.75×9.75−2×9.75×5.75+5.75×5.75=?
    a) 13.25   b) 3.625
    c) 4   d) 16

14. 3.5 + 21 × 1.3 = ?
    a) 7.28   b) 6.13
    c) 72.8   d) 30.8

15. $\dfrac{48 - 12 \times 3 + 9}{3 + 9 \div 3} = ?$
    a) 3   b) 1
    c) 3½   d) $\dfrac{1}{3}$

16. 171 ÷ 19 × 9 = ?
    a) 0   b) 1
    c) 18   d) 81

17. $\sqrt{256} \div \sqrt{x} = 2.$ x = ?
    a) 64   b) 128
    c) 512   d) 1024

18. $\dfrac{112}{\sqrt{196}} \times \dfrac{\sqrt{576}}{12} \times \dfrac{\sqrt{256}}{8} = ?$
    a) 8   b) 12
    c) 16   d) 32

19. ? % of 250 + 25% of 68 = 67
    a) 10   b) 15
    c) 20   d) 25

20. What is 25% of 25% equal to ?
    a) 6.25   b) .625
    c) .0625   d) .00625

21. Subtracting 6% of x from x is equivalent to multiplying x by how much?
    a) .94   b) 9.4
    c) .094   d) 94

22. $\sqrt{(3.6\% \text{ of } 40)} = ?$
    a) 2.8   b) 1.8
    c) 1.2   d) 1.1

23. If A : B = 2 : 3 , B : C = 4 : 5, C : D = 6 : 7, A : D = ?
    a) 2 : 7   b) 7 : 8
    c) 16 : 35   d) 4 : 13

24. 24 + (41 × 42)   = ?
    a) 1800   b) 1679
    c) 1872   d) None of these

25. 3.254 × 0.65 = ?
    a) 21.151   b) 2.1151
    c) .27215   d) .02725

• TEST No. 2 •

General Knowledge

1. Harsha followed
   a) Jainism
   b) Sikhism
   c) Buddhism
   d) Hinduism

2. Harshacharita was written by
   a) Banbhatt
   b) Harsha Vardhana
   c) Kalidas
   d) Jaidev

3. Who among the following was the only woman ruler to sit on the throne of Delhi?
   a) Chand Bibi
   b) Jahan Aara
   c) Nur Jahan
   d) Razia Sultana

4. Where did the British East India Company open its first factory in India?
   a) Madras (Chennai)
   b) Surat
   c) Calcutta (Kolkata)
   d) Bombay (Mumbai)

5. The famous king of Kushana dynasty was
   a) Kuvishka
   b) Kamarupa
   c) Kanishka
   d) Phisya

6. The enthronment of Kanishka coincides with
   a) Tamil Era
   b) Hindi Era
   c) Saka Era
   d) Bengali Era

7. The old name of Delhi was
   a) Pataliputra
   b) Ayodhya
   c) Gaya
   d) Indraprastha

8. Which of the following countries hosted the Olympic Games, 2008?
   a) USA
   b) China
   c) Japan
   d) Australia

9. Megasthanes was a/an
   a) Ambassador
   b) Traveller
   c) Ascetic
   d) Teacher

10. December 1 is celebrated every year as
    a) World Habitat Day
    b) World Children's Day
    c) World AIDS Day
    d) UN Day

11. The major establishments of Indian Space Research Organisation (ISRO) are located in the following three states, EXCEPT
    a) Kerala
    b) Karnataka
    c) Andhra Pradesh
    d) Maharashtra

12. December 15 is celebrated as Vijay Divas to commemorate
    a) First Revolt for Independence
    b) Freedom Proposal
    c) Victory over Pakistan in 1971
    d) Unification of UAE

13. Mohanjodaro and Harappa are in
    a) India
    b) Afghanistan
    c) Bangladesh
    d) Pakistan

14. Jainism was founded by
    a) Tirthangara
    b) Ukkirama Jain
    c) Mahavira
    d) Niravana

15. Where was the first session of Indian National Congress held?
    a) Bombay (Mumbai)
    b) Delhi
    c) Madras (Chennai)
    d) Calcutta (Kolkata)

16. Who invented Crescograph?
    a) J.C. Bose
    b) Niels Bohr
    c) Rutherford
    d) Albert Einstein

17. 'Land of Rising Sun' is called
    a) Vietnam
    b) Japan
    c) Australia
    d) China

18. Who is the author of the book 'A Tale of Two Cities'?
    a) D.H. Lawrence
    b) R.L. Stevenson
    c) Charles Dickens
    d) William Shakespeare

19. When is the UN Day celebrated?
    a) October 24
    b) January 24
    c) June 24
    d) September 24

20. Where is the Headquarters of the Indian Tobacco Company (ITC) located?
    a) Hyderabad
    b) Kolkata
    c) Mumbai
    d) Delhi

21. 'Long Walk to Freedom' is the autobiography of
    a) Martin Luther King
    b) Nelson Mandela
    c) Fidel Castro
    d) Farooq Abdullah

22. UN Secretary General Ban-Ki-moon belongs to which of the following countries?
    a) South Korea   b) Ghana
    c) Congo   d) Kenya

23. The term 'Tee' is associated with which of the following sports?
    a) Golf   b) Table Tennis
    c) Polo   d) Judo

24. 'Beating the Retreat' ceremony is associated with
    a) Republic Day   b) Martyrs' Day
    c) Labour Day   d) Independence Day

25. At which of the following places is the maximum concentration of uranium found in India?
    a) Jharia   b) Keonjhar
    c) Singhbhum   d) Siliguri

Reasoning - General Intelligence

Directions (Qns. 1-5): In the following questions, three classes are given. Out of the four response figures, you are to indicate which figure will best represent the relationship amongst the three classes

    (a)   (b)   (c)   (d)

1. Women, Mothers, Widows
    (a)   (b)   (c)   (d)
2. Writer, Teacher, Men
    (a)   (b)   (c)   (d)
3. Sparrow, Bird, Mouse
    (a)   (b)   (c)   (d)
4. Tea, Coffee, Beverages
    (a)   (b)   (c)   (d)
5. Boy, Student, Gymnast
    (a)   (b)   (c)   (d)

6. One quantity of water in a tank doubles every minute. It gets filled in 60 minutes. In how many minutes will it be half-filled?
    a) 20   b) 30
    c) 40   d) 59

7. What is the minimum number of ducks which can swim in the following manner? Two ducks are in front of one duck and one duck is between two ducks.
    a) 11   b) 9
    c) 7   d) 3

Directions (Qns. 8-12): Find the ODD man out.

8. 5, 7, 9, 17, 23, 37
    a) 5   b) 9
    c) 37   d) 23

9. a) Patience   b) Vacation
   c) Kindness   d) Steamer

10. a) Darjeeling   b) Shimla
    c) Delhi   d) Nainital

11. a) Earth   b) Moon
    c) Venus   d) Mars

12. a) Pearl   b) Topaz
    c) Diamond   d) Ruby

Directions (Qns.13-20) : Find the missing number in each of the following questions.

13. 1, 4, 9, 25, 36, ...?
    a) 48   b) 49
    c) 52   d) 56

14. 6, 11, 21, 36, 56,..............?
    a) 66   b) 76
    c) 81   d) 86

15. 3, 7, 15, 31, 63, ... ?
    a) 92   b) 115
    c) 127   d) 131

16. 0, 2, 8, 14, 24, 34, ... ?
    a) 48   b) 42
    c) 40   d) 36

17. 19, 2, 38, 3, 114, 4, ... ?
    a) 228   b) 256
    c) 356   d) 456

18. 2, 15, 41, 80, 132, ... ?
    a) 145   b) 165
    c) 181   d) 197

19. 2, 3, 8, 63, ... ?
    a) 1038   b) 3008
    c) 3968   d) 3268

20. 840, 168, 42, 14, 7, ...?
    a) 7   b) 5
    c) 3   d) 1

Directions. (Qns. 21-25): Choose the alternative which have the same relationship in the third term as is between first and second terms.

21. **Moon : Satellite : : Earth : ?**
    a) Sun
    b) Planet
    c) Galaxy
    d) Asteroid

22. **Flower : Bud : : Plant : ?**
    a) Seed
    b) Fruit
    c) Flower
    d) Stem

23. **Car : Garage : : Aeroplane : ?**
    a) Airport
    b) Depot
    c) Hanger
    d) Port

24. **Chromate : Chromium :: Ilmenite : ?**
    a) Lime
    b) Cobalt
    c) Manganese
    d) Titanium

25. **Sphetic : Radio :: Gypsum : ?**
    a) Glass
    b) Porcelain
    c) Cement
    d) Powder

General English

1. Fill in the blank with suitable preposition:
   I saw Mohan talking _____ a stranger.
   a) for
   b) at
   c) to
   d) through

2. Select the correct question tag:
   Everyone is present, _____?
   a) isn't it
   b) weren't it
   c) didn't it
   d) don't it

3. Select the correct question tag:
   She sings sweetly, _____?
   a) don't she
   b) doesn't she
   c) willn't she
   d) didn't she

4. Select the correct question tag:
   All agreed to our plan, _____?
   a) didn't they
   b) didn't we
   c) didn't he
   d) didn't I

5. Select the correct question tag:
   He hasn't got a car, _____?
   a) does he
   b) doesn't he
   c) has he
   d) hasn't he

6. Match the following words given in Column A with their meanings in Column B and select the correct answer from the codes given below:

	Column A			Column B
A)	Ceased		1.	excited
B)	Battered		2.	unyieldingly
C)	Tensed		3.	beat hard
D)	Stubbornly		4.	stopped

	A	B	C	D
a)	4	3	1	2
b)	3	4	2	1
c)	1	2	3	4
d)	2	1	4	3

7. Match the following phrases given in Column A with their meanings in Column B and select the correct answer from the codes given below:

Column A		Column B
A) held up	1.	postponed
B) backed up	2.	tolerate
C) put off	3.	delayed
D) put on	4.	supported
E) put up	5.	wear

	A	B	C	D	E
a)	3	4	1	5	2
b)	3	1	2	5	4
c)	4	5	1	2	3
d)	5	1	4	3	2

8. Match the following words and phrases given in Column A with their meanings in Column B and select the correct answer from the codes given below:

Column A		Column B
A) distrust	1.	start
B) spoil	2.	failure
C) take off	3.	doubt
D) break down	4.	damage

	A	B	C	D
a)	4	1	2	3
b)	1	2	3	4
c)	2	3	4	1
d)	3	4	1	2

9. Match the following words given in Column A with their meanings in Column B and select the correct answer from the codes given below:

Column A		Column B
A) cheering		1. defeat completely
B) checkmate		2. deep thought
C) meditation		3. happy
D) weather		4. climate

	A	B	C	D
a)	4	2	3	1
b)	3	1	4	2
c)	1	2	4	3
d)	3	1	2	4

10. Match the following words and phrases given in Column A with their meanings in Column B and select the correct answer from the codes given below:

Column A	Column B
A) condemn	1. visit casually
B) inevitably	2. punish
C) go through	3. unavoidably
D) drop in	4. examine

	A	B	C	D
a)	3	1	4	2
b)	1	4	2	3
c)	2	3	4	1
d)	2	3	1	4

11. Match the following words and phrases given in Column A with their meanings in Column B and select the correct answer from the codes given below:

Column A	Column B
A) absolute	1. freedom
B) marvellous	2. come up
C) liberty	3. limitless
D) turn up	4. wonderful

	A	B	C	D
a)	3	2	1	4
b)	3	4	1	2
c)	1	4	3	2
d)	3	4	2	1

12. Choose the correct 'synonym' for the italicized word from the options given:

Mr. John has a good *reputation* as a doctor.

a) reference
b) respect
c) fame
d) remark

13. Choose the correct 'synonym' for the italicized word from the options given:

The student is taught unarmed *combat.*

a) fight
b) quarrel
c) war
d) race

14. Choose the correct 'synonym' for the italicized word from the options given:

Einstein's *domestic* life was pathetic.

a) personal
b) married
c) family
d) public

15. Choose the correct 'synonym' for the italicized word from the options given:

The shocking news *reverberated* round the world.

a) shocked
b) echoed
c) sounded
d) surrounded

16. Find out the odd word:

a) involuntary
b) involuntarily
c) involve
d) invigilate

17. Find out the odd word:

a) condensation
b) condemnation
c) condemn
d) conciliation

18. Select the correct Plural form of "Calf":

a) calfs
b) calfes
c) calves
d) calf

19. Select the correct Plural form of "Information":

a) information
b) informations
c) informationes
d) informationses

20. Select the correct Plural form of "Mouse":

a) mouses
b) mice
c) mouse
d) mices

21. Select the correct Plural form of "Terminus":

a) terminuses
b) termini
c) terminious
d) terminioes

22. Select the correct Plural form of "Loaf":

a) loafs
b) loaves
c) loafes
d) loafes

23. Select the correct Plural form of "Oasis":

a) oasises
b) oases
c) oasiss
d) oasies

24. Identify the Complex sentence:

a) He worked hard to pass the Examination.
b) He worked hard so that he might pass the Examination.
c) He worked hard and passed the Examination.
d) To pass the Examination he worked hard.

25. Identify the following sentence:

He could not continue his studies as he fell ill.

a) simple
b) complex
c) compound
d) none

Arithmetic - Numerical Ability

1. The population of a town increased from 4000 to 6000. Find the percentage of increase.
   a) 50%
   b) 30%
   c) 20%
   d) 40%

2. The students strength of a school was 840 last year. This year, there is an increase of 10%. Find the present strength of students.
   a) 824
   b) 848
   c) 924
   d) 948

3. A boy scored 130 marks out of 150. Find the percentage of his mark.
   a) $86.\overline{6}$
   b) $83.\overline{3}$
   c) $85.\overline{1}$
   d) $87.\overline{5}$

4. Find the value of $\dfrac{(85 \times 85) - (25 \times 25)}{(85 + 25)}$
   a) 60
   b) 40
   c) 45
   d) 50

5. Which of the following numbers is the largest?
   a) $(2 + 2 + 2)^2$
   b) $\{(2 + 2)^2\}^2$
   c) $(2 \times 2 \times 2)^2$
   d) $(2 + 2)^2 + (2)^2$

6. If 16 workers can finish a job in 3 hours, how long would it take for 5 workers to finish the same job?
   a) $1\dfrac{1}{2}$ hours
   b) $5\dfrac{1}{2}$ hours
   c) $2\dfrac{1}{16}$ hours
   d) $9\dfrac{3}{5}$ hours

7. If a tray contains 6 red socks and 4 blue socks, what is the probability that 2 socks, picked will be red?
   a) $\dfrac{2}{15}$
   b) $\dfrac{4}{15}$
   c) $\dfrac{1}{3}$
   d) $\dfrac{2}{5}$

8. What is $\dfrac{1}{2}$ of $\dfrac{x}{2}$?
   a) $\dfrac{1}{x}$
   b) $\dfrac{1}{4}$
   c) $\dfrac{x}{4}$
   d) $4 \ x$

9. $1\dfrac{1}{4}$ (x) $= \dfrac{1}{2}$. Find the value of x.
   a) $\dfrac{2}{5}$
   b) $\dfrac{5}{8}$
   c) $1\dfrac{3}{5}$
   d) $2\dfrac{1}{2}$

10. Mr. A is now x–10 years old. How old will he be 10 years from now?
    a) x – 20
    b) x + 10
    c) x
    d) x + 20

11. When 75% of a number is added to 75, the result is the number again. Find the number.
    a) 350
    b) 300
    c) 250
    d) 200

12. The volume of a cylinder is 4158 cm³. Its diameter is 21 cm. Find its total surface area.
    a) 1485
    b) 1265
    c) 1375
    d) 1595

13. The diameter of a cone is 1.4 cm. Its slant height is 4.2 cm. Find curved surface area.
    a) 9.24 cm²
    b) 2.24 cm²
    c) 8.14 cm²
    d) 6.94 cm²

14. The radius of a cone is 10.5 cm and its height is 14 cm. Find the slant height l.
    a) 17.5 cm
    b) 21.5 cm
    c) 23.5 cm
    d) 15.5 cm

15. Find the curved surface area of a cone with a radius of 4.9 cm and a slant height 'l' of 14 cm.
    a) 225.6 cm²
    b) 235.6 cm²
    c) 215.6 cm²
    d) 245.6 cm²

16. How many litres of water can be stored in a hemisphere of radius 10.5 dm?
    a) 3465 lit
    b) 2425.5 lit
    c) 2465.5 lit
    d) 3425 lit

17. Calculate the Curved Surface Area (C.S.A.) of a hemisphere whose radius is 1.75 cm.
    a) 20.25 cm²
    b) 19.25 cm²
    c) 21.25 cm²
    d) 22.25 cm²

18. Find Total Surface Area (T.S.A.) of a hemisphere of diameter 20 cm.
   a) 842.86 cm^2 b) 886.26 cm^2
   c) 942.86 cm^2 d) 996.26 cm^2

19. Calculate the surface area of a sphere whose radius is 21 cm.
   a) 5544 cm^2 b) 6622 cm^2
   c) 7733 cm^2 d) 4455 cm^2

20. The total surface area of a sphere is 154 cm^2. Its radius is 3.5 cm. Find its volume.
   a) 169.77 cm^3 b) 189.07 cm^3
   c) 159.27 cm^3 d) 179.67 cm^3

21. A cone has a radius of 3 cm and slant height of 5 cm. Its vertical height is
   a) $\sqrt{3^2 + 5^2}$ b) $5^2 - 3^2$
   c) $3^2 + 5^2$ d) $\sqrt{5^2 - 3^2}$

22. Write 0.00452 in scientific notation.
   a) 4.52×10^{-3}
   b) 452×10^{-5}
   c) 0.452×10^{-2}
   d) 45.2×10^{-3}

23. Write 4783 in standard form.
   a) 4783.0
   b) 4,783
   c) 4.783×10^3
   d) 4.783×1000

24. Simplify $x^4 \times x^3$
   a) x^{4-3} b) x
   c) $x^{4 \times 3}$ d) x^7

25. $y^7 \div y = ?$
   a) y^7 b) y^6
   c) y^5 d) $y^{7 \times 1}$

TEST No. 3

General Knowledge

1. Kanishka followed
   a) Jainism   b) Sikhism
   c) Buddhism   d) Hinduism

2. Indian Napoleon was
   a) Chandra Gupta I   b) Chandra Gupta II
   c) Samudra Gupta   d) Skanda Gupta

3. Swadeshi Steam Navigation Company was founded by
   a) Tilak   b) Gandhiji
   c) V.O.Chidambaram   d) Rajaji

4. Who among the following explained that the earth moves round the sun?
   a) Aryabhatta   b) Vatsyayana
   c) Susruta   d) Vishnugupta

5. Kurukshetra is modern
   a) Delhi   b) Panipat
   c) Sonepet   d) Faridabad

6. The play 'Malavikagnimitram' was written by
   a) Kalidasa   b) Chanakya
   c) Chandragupta Maurya
   d) Kalhana

7. The language used during Sangam period was
   a) Telugu   b) Malayalam
   c) Tamil   d) Sanskrit

8. Solar eclipse occurs when
   a) Earth is between the Sun and the Moon
   b) Moon is between the Sun and the Earth
   c) Sun is between the Earth and the Moon
   d) None of these

9. Indian Standard Time (I.S.T.) is the local time of
   a) Delhi   b) Chennai
   c) Allahabad   d) Kolkata

10. Pampas are
   a) tropical grass lands
   b) tracks full of trees
   c) vast plains
   d) mountains

11. Delhi is on the banks of
   a) Ganges
   b) Sutlej
   c) Tapti
   d) Yamuna

12. Lignite is found in
    a) Muzaffarpur   b) Kilar
    c) Neyveli   d) Kolar

13. Ajanta caves are situated in
    a) Maharashtra   b) Andhra Pradesh
    c) Uttar Pradesh   d) Tamil Nadu

14. Kangaroo is found in
    a) Australia   b) New Zealand
    c) Japan   d) India

15. Emu is a
    b) bird   b) animal
    c) ape-man   d) Train

16. The first man to set foot on the moon was
    a) Edwin Aldrin
    b) Neil Armstrong
    c) Collins
    d) Leonard

17. The first woman to enter space was
    a) Yuri Gagarin   b) Leonav
    c) Tereshkova   d) Collus

18. Taj Mahal is built on the banks of the river
    a) Ganges   b) Sind
    c) Brahmaputra   d) Jamuna

19. The river Cauvery flows from
    a) Karnataka to Tamil Nadu
    b) Karnataka to Maharashtra
    c) Andhra to Tamil Nadu
    d) Kerala to Tamil Nadu

20. The largest city in India is
    a) Mumbai   b) Kolkata
    c) Delhi   d) Bangalore

21. Teachers' day is celebrated every year on
    a) 26th November   b) 5th September
    c) 20th October   d) 2nd November

22. Mahatma Gandhi's mother's name is
    a) Devaki   b) Putlibai
    c) Yesotha   d) None

23. 'Roentgen' discovered
    a) X-rays   b) Encephalograph
    c) Anti-Polio Vaccine   d) None of these

24. 'Television' was invented by
    a) Sholes   b) Shockley
    c) J.L.Baird   d) None of them

25. 'Helicopter' was invented by
    a) Broquet   b) Cockrell
    c) Drinker   d) None of them

Reasoning - General Intelligence

1. Supply the missing figure:

    $$\frac{5}{10} \times \frac{8}{7} \times \frac{100}{50} \times \frac{35}{40} \times \frac{?}{16} = \frac{1}{8}$$

    a) 2   b) 4
    c) 8   d) 16

2. A chair is sold at a profit of 10% for Rs. 220. Find the cost price.
    a) Rs. 200   b) Rs. 210
    c) Rs. 180   d) Rs. 240

3. If one-fourth of a number is 72, then what will be its two-third?
    a) 54   b) 64
    c) 96   d) 192

4. A sum of Rs. 1,000 at interest compounded annually amounts to Rs. 1,331 in 3 years. Find the rate of interest.
    a) 8%   b) 10%
    c) 12%   d) 7%

5. Complete the series: 81, 69, 58, 48, 39, ...
    a) 7   b) 10
    c) 22   d) 31

6. I am tenth in the queue from either end. How many people are there in the queue?
    a) 13   b) 12
    c) 19   d) 10

7. Write the next number in the series: 14, 16, 13, 17, 12, 18, 11, ...
    a) 12   b) 19
    c) 22   d) 14

8. A Shepherd had 17 sheep. All but nine died. How many did he have left?
    a) 9   b) 8
    c) 12   d) 7

9. Supply the missing figure: 1, 4, 9, 16, 25, ..., 49
    a) 27   b) 36
    c) 64   d) 81

10. Supply the missing figure: 3, 11, 8, 16, 13, ..., **18**
    a) 15   b) 17
    c) 14   d) 21

11. Insert the missing number:

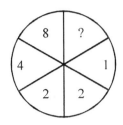

    a) 32   b) 8
    c) 16   d) 4

12. Answer in a short-cut method $(999)^2$
    a) 19848   b) 108431
    c) 93670   d) 998001

13. Write the next number in the series: 2, 5, 4, 9, 8, 15, ...
    a) 14   b) 27
    c) 81   d) 36

14. Complete the sequence: **Hare : Tortoise ::**
    a) telegram : letter   b) thesis : essay
    c) numbers : words   d) egotism : modesty

15. Today is Saturday, what day of the week will be after 27 days?
    a) Monday   b) Friday
    c) Wednesday   d) Saturday

16. Find the odd man out:
    a) Tree   b) Plant
    c) Grass   d) Stone

17. Find the odd man out:
    a) Christmas   b) Diwali
    c) Holi   d) Tuesday

18. Find the odd man out:
    a) East   b) West
    c) Best   d) North

19. Insert the missing number:

    12 [540] 4   27 [729] 5   8 [?] 4
        15   5   8
    a) 120   b) 240
    c) 64   d) 128

20. Doctor is to Medicine as Teacher is to
    a) books   b) education
    c) school   d) teaching

21. Think of a number; divide it by 4 and add 9 to it, the result is 15. Find the number.
    a) 20   b) 22
    c) 24   d) None of these

22. Find the odd man out:
    a) Patience   b) Vacation
    c) Kindness   d) Steamer

23. Find the odd man out:
    a) Darjeeling   b) Simla
    c) Delhi   d) Nainital

24. Find the odd man out:
    a) Earth   b) Moon
    c) Venus   d) Mars

25. Find the odd man out:
    a) Pearl   b) Topaz
    c) Diamond   d) Ruby

General English

Choose the correct word or phrase

1. He left for Mumbai by the ..... train.
    a) half past eight   b) eight-thirty
    c) eighty-thirty o' clock
    d) thirty minutes past eight

2. How did he kill the tiger? He killed it ..... a rifle.
    a) with   b) through
    c) from   d) by

3. This tea is cold. Please .... it.
    a) heat   b) warm
    c) fire   d) none of these

4. As he ..... the tap, water gushed out.
    a) opened
    b) turned around
    c) turned on   d) none of these

5. I wish I ..... a King.
    a) was   b) am
    c) should be   d) were

6. The city was plunged ..... darkness due to a sudden power failure.
    a) at   b) through
    c) to   d) into

Supply suitable prepositions from the given ones (where needed) in the blank spaces in the following sentences. If a preposition is not needed, tick 'd'

7. The party comprises ..... Ram, Mohan, Sita and myself.
   a) for
   b) of
   c) in
   d) none

8. The police wrongly charged him ..... murder.
   a) for
   b) of
   c) with
   d) none

9. Don't bother ..... these trivial matters.
   a) in
   b) on
   c) about
   d) none

10. I am fed up ..... staying at this place.
    a) at
    b) on
    c) with
    d) none

11. Mrs. and Mr. Sharma have been in Kanpur ..... last August.
    a) from
    b) since
    c) on
    d) none

12. Which hand do you write ..... ?
    a) with
    b) on
    c) in
    d) none

Fill in the spaces given below so as to make the verb and subject to agree:

13. The howling of your dogs _____ me.
    a) annoys
    b) annoy
    c) annoyed
    d) annexed

14. The snow of the moutains ___ spring.
    a) melt
    b) melts
    c) meets
    d) melted

15. ____ one of the best soaps I have ever used.
    a) This is
    b) These were
    c) That was
    d) That is

16. Four people ____ the movie.
    a) see
    b) saw
    c) sees
    d) seen

17. None of the players _____ known to me.
    a) is
    b) are
    c) been
    d) none

Qns. 18-21: Choose the word which is opposite in meaning to the word given in capitals.

18. WEARY
    a) Tired
    b) Haste
    c) Waste
    d) Jolly

19. DISPARAGE
    a) Justify
    b) Criticise
    c) Censure
    d) Legally

20. DISCIPLINE
    a) Order
    b) Systematic
    c) Indiscipline
    d) Standing

21. BEAUTIFUL
    a) Good
    b) Attractive
    c) Ugly
    d) Fine

Qns. 22-25: Choose the word which is nearly the same in meaning as the word given in capitals.

22. ANNEX
    a) Add
    b) Low
    c) Copy
    d) Initial

23. PRECINCT
    a) Delay
    b) Fear
    c) Oppose
    d) Vicinity

24. CONGREGATION
    a) Association
    b) Progress
    c) Cry
    d) Weeping

25. MANSION
    a) Polish
    b) Forward
    c) Large residence
    d) Office

Arithmetic - Numerical Ability

1. Add:

2	6	4	7	6
7	8	2	3	4
9	7	4	6	2
3	8	6	4	3

   a) 2401815
   b) 234715
   c) 240815
   d) 294805

2. $\sqrt{441} =$
   a) 21
   b) ± 21
   c) 29
   d) 20.9

3. $3/4 + 7/8 + 1/6 = ?$
   a) 9/12
   b) 7/12
   c) 5/24
   d) none of these

4. $.1 \times .01 \times .001 = ?$
   a) .1
   b) .0001
   c) .001
   d) none of these

5. $\dfrac{3.92}{.8} = ?$
   a) .4
   b) .44
   c) .044
   d) none of these

6. $\dfrac{1}{3} \times \dfrac{5}{6} \times \dfrac{7}{8} \times \dfrac{8}{9} =$
   a) 35/162
   b) 34/161
   c) 4/61
   d) 5/72

7. $\dfrac{2}{3} \times \dfrac{5}{8} \times \dfrac{3}{9} \times \dfrac{1}{6} =$
   a) 7/216
   b) 12/286
   c) 5/216
   d) 9/216

8. $\dfrac{.4 \times .5 \times .6 \times .7}{1 \times 2 \times 3} =$
   a) .14
   b) 0.104
   c) 0.014
   d) 10.14

9. $\dfrac{2.3 \times 4.5 \times 6.7 \times 3.4}{2 \times 3 \times 4 \times 5}$
   a) $\dfrac{235.773}{120}$
   b) $\dfrac{127.334}{120}$
   c) $\dfrac{234.337}{120}$
   d) $\dfrac{137.43}{120}$

10. A person gets Rs. 300 as 1st year's interest on a certain sum and Rs.330 as 2nd year's interest. Find the sum.
    a) Rs.9000
    b) Rs.3000
    c) Rs.4000
    d) Rs.5000

11. A man buys 10 articles for Rs. 8 and sells the articles at the rate of 1.25 per article. His gain per cent is
    a) 50%
    b) 56¼%
    c) 20%
    d) 19½%

12. A man buys 16 litres of milk at Rs. 4.80 per litre and adds 4 litres of water. If he wants a profit of 12½%, at what rate should he sell the mixture?
    a) Rs. 4.32 per litre
    b) Rs. 5.00 per litre
    c) Rs. 4.60 per litre
    d) Rs. 3.80 per litre

13.
```
            9
          9 9
        9 9 9
      9 9 9 9
  +   9 9 9 9 9
```
    a) 100105
    b) 111805
    c) 111105
    d) 111115

14.
```
      7 7 7 7 7
  -   * * * * *
      5 8 4 7 9
```
    a) 19428
    b) 19298
    c) 19498
    d) 14998

15. $\sqrt{\dfrac{4}{5} \times \dfrac{9}{125}}$
    a) $\dfrac{18}{25}$
    b) $\dfrac{12}{125}$
    c) $\dfrac{6}{25}$
    d) 0.316

16. River A and River B have a combined length of 650 miles and River B is 250 miles shorter than River A. How many miles long is River B?
    a) 200
    b) 300
    c) 550
    d) 600

17. A certain sum of money amounts to Rs.770/- in one year and amounts to Rs.847 in two years at certain rate of interest. Find the sum.
    a) Rs.700
    b) Rs.600
    c) Rs.500
    d) Rs.400

18. A book contains 50 leaves. On each page there are 20 lines and in each line there are 10 words? How may words does that book contain?
    a) 10,000
    b) 15,000
    c) 20,000
    d) 25,000

19. 20 men can dig 40 holes in 60 days. So, 10 men can dig 20 holes in how many days?
    a) 30 days
    b) 60 days
    c) 75 days
    d) 90 days

20. Express 12.5 percent as a fraction
    a) $\dfrac{1}{4}$
    b) $\dfrac{1}{8}$
    c) $\dfrac{1}{16}$
    d) $\dfrac{1}{32}$

21. The length of a plot is twice its breadth. Its area is 4050 sq.m. Find the cost of fencing the plot at Rs.2.50 per metre.
    a) Rs. 525/-
    b) Rs. 675/-
    c) Rs. 415/-
    d) Rs. 652/-

22. If Rs. 91/- is divided among A, B, C in the ratio $1\frac{1}{2}$: $3\frac{1}{3}$: $2\frac{3}{4}$, B will get
    a) Rs. 36
    b) Rs. 40
    c) Rs. 45
    d) Rs. 48

23. In a triangle ABC, find Angle B, if Angles (B+C) = 130° and Angle A = Angle C
    a) 60°
    b) 70°
    c) 80°
    d) 50°

24. In a refugee camp there is enough food for 30 days for 20,000 persons. After 10 days, another 5,000 persons join in. If the ration to each is reduced by ½, for how many more days will the food available be sufficient?
    a) 25 days
    b) 30 days
    c) 15 days
    d) 32 days

25. The length and breadth of a room are in ratio 5:2. If length had been 8M. less and width 4M. more, the room would have been a square. What are the measurements of the room?
    a) Length 15 M; Breadth 2 M
    b) Length 18 M; Breadth 3 M
    c) Length 20 M; Breadth 8 M
    d) Length 16 M; Breadth 4 M

TEST No. 4

General Knowledge

1. The total number of Union Territories is
   a) 7
   b) 10
   c) 11
   d) 12

2. India is
   a) a Federation
   b) a Unitary State
   c) a Union of States
   d) Quasi-federal

3. The colours of our national flag from top are in the order of
   a) saffron, white and green
   b) green, white and saffron
   c) white, green and saffron
   d) saffron, green and white

4. The chakra in our national flag has
   a) 12 spokes
   b) 18 spokes
   c) 24 spokes
   d) 30 spokes

5. The famous king of Chola dynasty was
   a) Raja Raja I
   b) Nedunchezhiyan
   c) Pulekesin II
   d) Harsha

6. Kurukshetra is modern
   a) Delhi
   b) Panipat
   c) Sonepet
   d) Faridabad

7. Mahatma Gandhi was first called 'the Father of the Nation' by
   a) Jawaharlal Nehru
   b) Subhas Chandra Bose
   c) Vallabhbhai Patel
   d) C.Rajagopalachari

8. Lunar eclipse occurs when
   a) Earth is between the Sun and the Moon
   b) Moon is between the Sun and the Earth
   c) Sun is between the Earth and the Moon
   d) None of these

9. Chittaranjan is known for
   a) Fertilizers
   b) Penicillin Industry
   c) Railway Engine
   d) Oil

10. Bandipur Sanctuary is located in the State of
    a) Tamil Nadu
    b) Uttar Pradesh
    c) Karnataka
    d) Orissa

11. Konkani, the language included in the 8th Schedule of the Constitution in 1992, is widely spoken in which State/Union Territory?
    a) Goa
    b) Pondicherry
    c) Andaman and Nicobar
    d) Lakshadweep

12. Which vitamin is provided by sunlight to body?
    a) A
    b) B
    c) C
    d) D

13. Typewriter was invented by
    a) Shockley
    b) Sholes
    c) Howe
    d) None of these

14. 'Stethoscope' was invented by
    a) Bessemer
    b) Lainnec
    c) Becqueral
    d) None of these

15. The 'Solar System' was discovered by
    a) Galileo
    b) Copernicus
    c) Finsen
    d) None of these

16. During photosynthesis, plants need
    a) Oxygen
    b) Nitrogen
    c) Water
    d) Carbon dioxide

17. Horse-power is a unit of
    a) power
    b) electric current
    c) three-horses
    d) electricity

18. 'Angstrom' is a unit used to measure
    a) the wave-length of light
    b) the speed of rockets
    c) the energy
    d) None of these

19. 'Rickets' is caused due to lack of
    a) Vitamin-A
    b) Vitamin-B
    c) Vitamin-D
    d) None of these

20. 'Cataract' is the disease of
    a) ears
    b) legs
    c) eyes
    d) None of these

21. 'Haemoglobin' is found in
    a) blood
    b) bile fluid
    c) sweat
    d) None of these

22. The normal temperature of human body is
    a) 98.4°F
    b) 36.9°C
    c) –37°C
    d) 98.4°K

23. Where from 'Satyameva Jayate' is taken?
    a) Mundaka Upanishad
    b) Mahabharata
    c) Thirukkural
    d) Artha Shastra

24. The Prime Minister of India is
    a) Atal Behari Vajpayee
    b) Shankar Dayal Sharma
    c) Manmohan Singh
    d) Lal Krishna Advani

25. Harshacharita was written by
    a) Banbhatt
    b) Harsha Vardhana
    c) Kalidas
    d) Jaidev

Reasoning - General Intelligence

1. Insert the missing number: 1, 2, 5, 12, ...
   a) 24
   b) 27
   c) 10
   d) 25

2. Answer in a short-cut method: 709 + 333 + 222 + 111 + 99 + 88 + 77 + 66 + 55 + 44 + 33 + 22 + 11 + 1 = ?
   a) 3,001
   b) 1,034
   c) 1,997
   d) 1,871

3. Complete the series: 2, 5, 9, 12, 16, 19, ...
   a) 24
   b) 23
   c) 32
   d) 28

Directions (Qns. 4 & 5): Find the next number in the series:

4. 8, 0, 15, 9, 22, 18, 29, 27, ...
   a) 63
   b) 127
   c) 243
   d) 36

5. 24, 72, 36, 108, 54, 162, ...
   a) 63
   b) 227
   c) 243
   d) 81

6. Insert the missing number:

   a) 9
   b) 34
   c) 33
   d) 35

7. Find out the number, which when divided by 4 and added by 9 gives the answer 15?
   a) 21
   b) 26
   c) 24
   d) 22

Directions (Qns. 8-10): In the following Questions three words have been given which have some common quality to them. This common quality is given as one of the four alternatives under it. Find out the correct alternative:

8. **Cap, Coat, Trousers**
   a) hair
   b) dress
   c) turban
   d) umbrella

9. **January, June, July**
   a) Rainy Season
   b) Summer
   c) Month
   d) March

10. **Cheese, Curd, Butter**
    a) Ghee   b) White
    c) Milk   d) Cow

11. **Of the following the one that is not equivalent to 376 is:**
    a) $(2 \times 100) + (17 \times 10) + 6$
    b) $(3 \times 100) + (7 \times 10) + 6$
    c) $(2 \times 106) + (16 \times 10) + 106$
    d) $(2 \times 100) + (7 \times 10) + 106$

12. **What per cent is 14 of 23?**
    a) 60%   b) $61\frac{1}{2}$ %
    c) $60\frac{2}{3}$ %   d) $60\frac{1}{3}$ %

13. **Insert the missing number: 514, 258, 130, 66, ...**
    a) 34   b) 33
    c) 36   d) 38

14. **Find the odd man out: 225, 289, 400, 36, 35**
    a) 225   b) 400
    c) 35   d) 36

15. **Ramu has 60 one rupee currency notes which bear numbers in order. If the number of the first note is 7575, find the number of the last note.**
    a) 7635   b) 7632
    c) 7633   d) 7634

16. **Find two numbers whose sum is 26 and difference 4. Mark the lower of them.**
    a) 10   b) 24
    c) 4   d) 11

17. **How many 7s are there in the full sequence which are followed by 3 but not preceded by 9?**
    4 3 7 9 1 6 7 3 9 5 4 9 7 3 5 3 7 3
    1 6 7 3 6 9 9 7 3 4 8 3
    a) 2   b) 3
    c) 4   d) 5

18. **Write the next number in the series: 14, 16, 13, 17, 12, 18, 11 .....**
    a) 12   b) 19
    c) 22   d) 14

19. **If A = 1, B = 3, C = 5 and so on, what do the numbers 3, 9, 7 stand for?**
    a) BID   b) BAD
    c) BED   d) CAR

20. **Which is the number if it comes to 15 when divided by 4 and added by 9?**
    a) 21   b) 26
    c) 24   d) 22

21. **If**   53 − 34 = 5334
            64 − 56 = 6546
    then 75 − 24 = ?
    a) 7524   b) 7452
    c) 7542   d) 7254

Find the next number in the series from questions 22 to 25:

22. **2.4, 5.3, 8.2, 11.1,?**
    a) 12.1   b) 14.2
    c) 14   d) 15.1

23. **1, 2, 5, 16, ?**
    a) 67   b) 30
    c) 65   d) 50

24. **10, 12, 32, 34, 54, 56, ?**
    a) 58   b) 60
    c) 76   d) 61

25. **15, 52, 26, 63, 37, ?**
    a) 20   b) 70
    c) 55   d) none of these

General English

Choose the correct word or phrase:

1. **I'll come to meet you at the station in my car _____ you do not have to walk to my house.**
   a) so that   b) in order
   c) that   d) because

2. **My father _____ me that I should have informed him.**
   a) said
   b) told
   c) asked
   d) none

3. My little daughter is not afraid of going in the dark alone. She is very _____
   a) brave
   b) strong
   c) healthy
   d) none

4. The student _____ that book from the library to study at home.
   a) issued
   b) borrowed
   c) hired
   d) lent

5. Can you pay _____ all these articles?
   a) for
   b) of
   c) off
   d) out

Supply suitable prepositions from the given ones (where needed) in the blank spaces in the following sentences:

6. The police wrongly charged him _____ murder.
   a) for
   b) of
   c) with
   d) none

7. Mrs. and Mr. Sharma have been in Kanpur _____ last August.
   a) from
   b) since
   c) on
   d) none

8. Which hand do you write _____?
   a) with
   b) on
   c) in
   d) about

9. How did you cut your finger? I _____ it with a knife.
   a) had cut
   b) have cut
   c) was cut
   d) cut

Pick out the correct collective noun from the words given:

10. A _____ of stars were shining in the sky.
    a) galaxy
    b) group
    c) pack
    d) set

11. The hunter had a ____ of arrows in his quiver.
    a) bunch
    b) set
    c) sheaf
    d) faggot

12. The artist arranged an exhibition of a _____ of his pictures.
    a) flight
    b) group
    c) gallery
    d) parade

13. A _____ of bees attacked the people in the park.
    a) flight
    b) sheaf
    c) swarm
    d) flock

14. Hampi is now a _____ of ruins.
    a) group
    b) crowd
    c) heap
    d) galaxy

In the words given below if the spelling is correct, put 'c', if wrong, put 'w':

15. recommend
16. occurence
17. exhilarate
18. grammar
19. drunkeness
20. procede

Choose (a) or (b) whichever is right in spelling:

21. a) baloon
    b) balloon
22. a) truely
    b) truly
23. a) asistant
    b) assistant
24. a) parallel
    b) paralell
25. a) Satelite
    b) Satellite

Arithmetic - Numerical Ability

1. If Rs.1,440 is divided into two parts in which one part is $\frac{7}{9}$ of the second, then the smallest part is
   a) Rs. 810
   b) Rs. 630
   c) Rs. 405
   d) Rs. 1,035

2. An article was sold at a loss of 29%. Had it been sold for Rs.84 more, 11% would have been gained; the cost price of that article is
   a) Rs. 210
   b) Rs. 200
   c) Rs. 180
   d) Rs. 170

3. In a $\triangle ABC$, AB=AC=2.5 cm, BC=4 cm. Find its height from A to the opposite base.
   a) 1.5 cm
   b) 1 cm
   c) 2 cm
   d) 3 cm

4. Price of 5 chairs and 2 tables is Rs.1350. Two chairs cost as much as one table. What is the price of one chair and one table?
   a) Rs. 450
   b) Rs. 350
   c) Rs. 500
   d) Rs. 550

5. Average of 6 numbers is 8, what number should be added to it to make the average 9?
   a) 15
   b) 16
   c) 17
   d) 18

6. The H.C.F. of two numbers is 11 and their L.C.M. is 7700. If one of the numbers is 275, the other is
   a) 279
   b) 283
   c) 308
   d) 318

7. The cost of 125 shirts is Rs. 11,250 and transportation charges are Rs. 375. For a 20% profit, the selling price of each shirt should be
   a) Rs. 111.60
   b) Rs. 112.00
   c) Rs. 112.50
   d) Rs. 111.50

8. 40 is what percent of 1200?
   a) 3
   b) $3\frac{1}{3}$
   c) $6\frac{2}{3}$
   d) 6

9. $\dfrac{\dfrac{1}{2}+\dfrac{3}{5}+\dfrac{6}{7}+\dfrac{8}{9}}{\dfrac{1}{2}+\dfrac{1}{2}} =$
   a) $\dfrac{1}{630}$
   b) $\dfrac{1793}{630}$
   c) $\dfrac{17}{630}$
   d) $\dfrac{13}{60}$

10.
3	*	*	8
–	3	0	4
3	1	3	4

   a) 54
   b) 42
   c) 37
   d) 43

11. $\dfrac{\sqrt{0.16}}{?} = 1$
   a) 0.4
   b) 0.04
   c) 0.8
   d) 0.08

12. There are 30 boys in a class and the average age is 15.1 years. Three new boys are put in this class, which made the average age 15.2 years. One new boy is aged 16 years the other two are twins. How old are the twins?
   a) 14
   b) 16.3
   c) 17
   d) 18

13. The property of a man was divided among his wife, son and daughter according to his 'will' as follows: wife's share is equal to $\frac{6}{7}$ of son's share and daughter's share is equal to $\frac{4}{7}$ of son's. If the son and daughter together receive Rs.1,02,300 how much does the wife get?
   a) Rs. 55,800
   b) Rs. 42,800
   c) Rs. 44,640
   d) Rs. 54,254

14. $\dfrac{60000 - 60^2}{160 - 60} =$
   a) 546
   b) 564
   c) 56.4
   d) 400

15. $1\frac{1}{2} + 2\frac{3}{4} + 4\frac{3}{8} =$
   a) $\dfrac{13}{8}$
   b) $8\frac{1}{2}$
   c) $7\frac{5}{8}$
   d) $8\frac{5}{8}$

16. A earns 10% more than B, but 15% less than C. If B earns Rs.85/-, then C earns
   a) Rs. 100/-
   b) Rs. 105/-
   c) Rs. 25/-
   d) Rs. 110/-

17. Rs. 6 is divided among A, B and C so that A gets 59p more than B and 53p less than C. Then A gets
   a) Rs. 2
   b) Rs. 2.02
   c) Rs. 2.05
   d) Rs. 1.98

18. $6\frac{4}{7} + 8\frac{2}{5} - 5\frac{3}{4} = ?$
   a) $9\frac{5}{7}$
   b) $8\frac{31}{140}$
   c) $9\frac{3}{14}$
   d) $9\frac{31}{140}$

19. A chair and a table together cost Rs. 100. If the chair costs Rs.16 less than the table, the cost of the table is
   a) Rs. 42
   b) Rs. 84
   c) Rs. 64
   d) Rs. 58

20. A certain number of 10 paise coins and thrice the number of 20 paise coins add up to Rs.21. If so, the number of 20 paise coins is
   a) 60
   b) 30
   c) 45
   d) 90

21. The 16th term of the series 1, 3, 6, 10, 15, ... is
   a) 132
   b) 136
   c) 126
   d) 120

22. A milk vendor buys 10 litres of milk at Rs. 4 per litre and adds 6 litres of water. If he wants a profit of 50%, at what rate he should sell this milk?
    a) Rs. 2.50   b) Rs. 3.75
    c) Rs. 4.50   d) Rs. 2.00

23. To a certain number 7 is added. The sum is multiplied by 5, the product is divided by 9 and 3 is subtracted from the quotient. If the remainder is 12, what is the number?
    a) 24   b) 20
    c) 40   d) 48

24. A can do a piece of work in 12 days, and B can do the same in 15 days. In how many days can both do it?

a) $5\dfrac{1}{2}$ b) $4\dfrac{1}{6}$

c) $6\dfrac{2}{3}$ d) $3\dfrac{1}{3}$

25. A + B can do a work in 6 days and the same work can be done by B + C in 10 days or C + A in 12 days. In how many days the three together can complete the work?

a) $2\dfrac{1}{2}$ b) $5\dfrac{5}{7}$

c) $3\dfrac{1}{6}$ d) $4\dfrac{1}{2}$

◦ TEST No. 5 ◦

General Knowledge

1. Name India's indigenously developed surface-to-air missile, successfully test-fired in November 2004.
   a) Akash   b) Dhanush
   c) BrahMos   d) Trishul

2. Nilgiri Mountain is in
   a) Karnataka   b) Tamil Nadu
   c) Rajasthan   d) Maharashtra

3. The largest city in India is
   a) Kolkata   b) Mumbai
   c) Delhi   d) Bangalore

4. Unit of electric current is
   a) Volt   b) Ampere
   c) Ohm   d) Watt

5. Who is the new U.S. Secretary of state?
   a) Mary Frances Bury b) Colin Powell
   c) Hillary Clinton   d) Dick Cheney

6. Name the company which has recently launched the third-generation mobile telephone services
   a) Vodafone   b) Nokia
   c) Samsung   d) Tata

7. The major component of honey is
   a) Glucose   b) Maltose
   c) Sucrose   d) Fructose

8. The oldest Veda is
   a) Rig Veda   b) Yajur Veda
   c) Sama Veda   d) Atharvana Veda

9. The traveller, who visited during the period of Harshavardhana was
   a) Hieun-tsang   b) Fahien
   c) Megasthanes   d) Roe

10. The last Governor-General was
    a) Rajaji   b) Lord Canning
    c) Warren Hastings   d) Lord Mountbatten

11. The Headquarters of UNO is at
    a) Washington   b) Geneva
    c) New York

12. Solar eclipse occurs when
    a) Earth is between the Sun and the Moon
    b) Moon is between the Sun and the Earth
    c) Sun is between the Earth and the Moon
    d) None of these

13. Corbett National Park is in the State of
    a) Madhya Pradesh   b) Assam
    c) Bihar   d) Uttarakhand

14. Earth revolves around the Sun in every
    a) 364   b) 365¼ days
    c) 365½ days   d) None of these

15. The First Asian to win Nobel Prize
    a) C.V. Raman   b) Vladimir Nabakov
    c) Rabindranath Tagore
    d) None of these

16. `Radar' is used to detect
    a) Flying objects   b) Military tanks
    c) Artilleries   d) None of these

17. An electric bulb makes a bang when it is broken because
    a) it has a partial vacuum
    b) a gas comes out of bulb
    c) the tungston makes the noise
    d) None of these

18. `Calorie' is the unit of
    a) Electricity   b) Light
    c) Heat   d) None of these

19. In an electric bulb, the filament is made of
    a) Copper   b) Tungsten
    c) Platinum   d) None of these

20. 'Bleeding of Gums' is caused due to lack of
    a) Vitamin-C   b) Vitamin-B
    c) Vitamin-A   d) None of these

21. 'Goitre' is caused due to lack of
    a) Iodine   b) Water
    c) White corpuscles   d) None of these

22. 'Rickets' is caused due to lack of
    a) Vitamin-A   b) Vitamin-B
    c) Vitamin-D   d) None of these

23. 'Malaria' is caused by
    a) Rats
    b) Anopheles mosquitoes
    c) Flies   d) None of these

24. Vitamin-C is richly found in
    a) Milk   b) Apple
    c) Lemon   d) None of these

25. Which planet is nearest to Earth?
    a) Pluto   b) Jupiter
    c) Venus   d) None of these

Reasoning - General Intelligence

1. Complete the series :
   11, 12, 17, 18, 23, 24 .....
   a) 30   b) 35
   c) 12   d) None of these

2. Complete the series :
   1, 8, 27, 64, 125, 216 .....
   a) 343   b) 512
   c) 729   d) 1000

3. Supply the missing figure:
   3, 11, 8, 16, 13 18
   a) 15   b) 17
   c) 14   d) 21

4. Which choice provides the answer: If $2+3=10$, $6+5=66$, $7+2=63$, $9+7=144$ then, $8+4=?$
   a) 48   b) 144
   c) 96   d) 55

5. Which choice provides the answer in the following: If $2 \times 3 = 36$, $5 \times 4 = 400$, $6 \times 2 = 144$, $3 \times 3 = 81$; then, $5 \times 5 = ?$
   a) 255
   b) 625
   c) 10
   d) 25

6. If $2 \times 8 = 4$, $3 \times 15 = 5$, $4 \times 24 = 6$, then $5 \times 40 = ?$
   a) 10   b) 8
   c) 6   d) 120

7. Four of the following numbers are alike in some way. Which one is not?
   19, 29, 21, 23, 13
   a) 23   b) 13
   c) 21   d) 29

8. Which choice provides the answer in the following: If $7+2=59$, $5+3=28$, $9+1= 810$, $2+1=13$, then $5+4=?$
   a) 19   b) 9
   c) 20   d) 239

9. Insert the missing letter
   A, D, G, J ......
   a) M   b) K
   c) L   d) F

10. Insert the missing number:

4	6	3	8
2	8	4	4
6	5	?	10

   a) 4   b) 3
   c) 8   d) 9

In the following questions 11 & 12, three words have been given which have some common quality to them. This common quality is given as one of the four alternatives under it. Find out the correct alternative.

11. Chennai, Mumbai, Kochi
    a) Port   b) Sea
    c) Kolkata   d) City

12. Sun, Earth, Mars
    a) Stars   b) Moon
    c) Solar System d) Sky

13. 1, 2, 5, 16, ?
    a) 67   b) 30
    c) 65   d) 50

14. 4, 7, 12, 19, 28, ?
    a) 39   b) 42
    c) 53   d) 21

15. Woodman : Axe : :
    a) Draftsman : Ruler   b) Painter : Brush
    c) Carpenter : Saw   d) Soldier : Gun

16. Cobra is to Snake as Crocodile is to
    a) Marsh   b) River
    c) Carnivore   d) Reptile

17. Fuel : Fire : :
    a) Gold : heat   b) Fire : forest
    c) Food : man   d) Wood : tree

18. Light is to Bright as Sun is to .....
    a) shine   b) heat
    c) burn   d) twinkle

19. Insert the missing number:
    175   (576)   463
    192   (   )   357
    a) 288   b) 82
    c) 330   d) 357

20. Think of a number; divide it by 4 and add 9 to it, the result is 15. Find the number.
    a) 20   b) 22
    c) 24   d) None of these

21. Doctor is to Medicine as Teacher is to ....
    a) books   b) education
    c) school   d) teaching

22. `Swarna' ranks 19th in a class of 49. What is her rank from the last?
    a) 19   b) 21
    c) 31   d) 30

23. If '+' means division, '−' means multiplication, '×' means minus, '÷' means plus, then (280 + 10 × 20) − 8 ÷ 6 is
    a) 70   b) 112
    c) −392   d) 58

In each of the following, five words have been given of which four are alike in some way and one is different. Choose out the ODD word.

24. a) Grape   b) Tomato
    c) Carrot   d) Beetroot   e) Banana

25. a) Ring   b) Locket
    c) Ornament   d) Ear ring   e) Bracelet

General English

Mark the part which has grammatical mistake:

1. He is / best boy / of his / class.
   a   b   c   d

2. If he / will come / I will / help him.
   a   b   c   d

3. He was one / of the greatest / poet of India.
   a   b   c

4. He / is too / weak.
   a   b   c

5. He is / one of the / most brilliant man.
   a   b   c

Select a word or phrase from the given list to complete the sentences.

6. He would not have failed if he .... enough money.
   a) would have   b) had had
   c) would have had d) was having

7. This is the first time I .... a typewriter.
   a) ever had used
   b) will ever use
   c) have ever been using
   d) have ever used

Supply suitable prepositions from the given ones (where needed) in the blank spaces in the following sentences.

8. Where did the police _____ their rifles?
    a) lay   b) laid
    c) lie   d) lied

9. When did you shoot the tiger?
    I _____ it last year.
    a) shoot   b) had shoot
    c) shot   d) have shot

Choose the correct word or phrase.

10. As he _____ the tap, water gushed out.
    a) opened   b) turned around
    c) turned on

11. The crime was _____ during the night.
    a) done   b) performed
    c) committed

Choose the most appropriate word from the set of words given under each sentence to fill the blank.

12. The victorious army _____ through the conquered city.
    a) loitered   b) strayed
    c) marched

13. I am _____ this examination in the hope of joining a Bank.
    a) completing   b) giving
    c) taking

Collective nouns : Pick out the correct nouns from the words given.

14. The Prime Minister was welcomed with garlands and a _____ of flowers.
    a) heap   b) bouquet
    c) crowd   d) swarm

15. The _____ of constables could not stand before the unruly crowd.
    a) group   b) troupe
    c) battalion   d) posse

Choose the word or phrase which is opposite in meaning to the key word.

16. **Ugly**
    a) repellent   b) uncomely
    c) attractive   d) clever

17. **Nasty**
    a) loathsome   b) inclement
    c) starry   d) clean

In the words given below if the spelling is correct, put 'C', if wrong put 'W'.

18. supersade   19. exceede

20. seperate   21. repitition

Tick (1) or (2) whichever you think is the correct form.

22. a) occurence   b) occurrence
23. a) pronounciation   b) pronunciation

Change the following sentences into indirect speech.

24. He said to me, "I shall give you a new pen".

25. He said, "I cut my finger".

Arithmetic - Numerical Ability

1. If 81 be divided in proportion of $\frac{1}{3}, \frac{1}{6}, \frac{1}{7}$, then the first part is,
    a) 36   b) 27
    c) 18   d) 42

2. If $\sqrt{625}$ is 25, then the value of $4 \div \sqrt{0.000625}$ will be
    a) 16.0   b) 0.160
    c) 160   d) 1600

3. x : 6 : : 32 : 24. What is the value of x?
    a) 7   b) 8
    c) 6   d) 5

4. Find the value of $\dfrac{(85 \times 85) - (25 \times 25)}{(85 + 25)}$
    a) 60   b) 40
    c) 45   d) 50

5. When 75% of a number is added to 75, the result is the number again. Find the number.
    a) 350   b) 300
    c) 250   d) 200

6. Find the H.C.F. of 24 and 30 from the following:
   a) 2   b) 4
   c) 6   d) 8

7. Find the L.C.M. of 6, 8 and 10.
   a) 24   b) 58
   c) 86   d) 120

8. 45% of x + 30% of 90 = 30% of 210. Then what is the value of x?
   a) 80   b) 85
   c) 90   d) 95

9. A person gets Rs.300/- as 1st year's interest on a certain sum and Rs.330/- as 2nd year's interest. Find the sum.
   a) Rs. 9000   b) Rs. 3000
   c) Rs. 4000   d) Rs. 5000

10. The compound interest on Rs.5,000 for two years at 4% is
    a) Rs. 400   b) Rs. 408
    c) Rs. 420   d) Rs. 440

11. Add:

    1 2 3 4 5 6 7 8 9
    9 8 7 6 5 4 3 2 1
    1 2 3 4 5 6 7 8 9
    9 8 7 6 5 4 3 2 1
    _____

    a) 222222220
    b) 222202220
    c) 42222222
    d) None of these

12. A has Rs. 120 less than B. C has Rs. 60 more than A. If all the three have Rs.1080 totally, the amount B has is
    a) Rs. 400   b) Rs. 380
    c) Rs. 420   d) Rs. 450

13. There are 5 numbers. The average of first four is 8 and the last four is 10. If the first number is 4, what is the last number?
    a) 20   b) 18
    c) 12   d) 10

14. $\dfrac{(27)^{n/3} \times (8)^{-n/6}}{(162)^{-n/2}}$
    a) 2^{3n} b) 3^{5n}
    c) 3^{3n} d) None of these

15. The average height of 40 students in a class was 160 cm. After 10 students join, the average became 156 cm. What is the total height of the 10 students newly joined?
    a) 1200 cm   b) 1400 cm
    c) 1100 cm   d) 1000 cm

16. A dealer marks his goods 25% above Cost Price and then while selling gives a discount of 12% on Market Price. What is his percentage of Profit?
    a) 20%   b) 30%
    c) 40%   d) 10%

17. A shop keeper sells 2 radios, each for Rs.600. If he gains 12% on one and suffers a loss of 12% on the other, what is his overall gain or loss?
    a) 1.25%   b) 1.35%
    c) 1.10% loss   d) 1.44% loss

18. A merchant sells goods for Rs. 900 and gains 12½%. If he wants a gain of 15%, for how much more he has to sell the goods?
    a) Rs. 20   b) Rs. 30
    c) Rs. 40   d) Rs. 10

19. A boat crosses a distance of 30 km in 5 Hrs downstream, and takes 6 Hrs to cover the same distance upstream. What is the speed of the boat? (or of current?)
    a) $2\dfrac{1}{2}$ b) $3\dfrac{1}{3}$
    c) $4\dfrac{1}{6}$ d) $5\dfrac{1}{2}$

20. The length and breadth of a rectangular field are in the ratio of 5 : 3. It's area is 1500 sq.mts. Find the cost of fencing the field at Re.1 per metre.
    a) Rs.400   b) Rs. 160
    c) Rs. 55   d) Rs. 80

21. The Simple Interest on a sum of money for $2\dfrac{1}{2}$ years at 6% per annum is more than the Simple Interest on the same money for $1\dfrac{1}{2}$ years at 8% per annum by Rs.18. What is the sum?
    a) Rs. 200   b) Rs. 300
    c) Rs. 400   d) Rs. 600

22. What is the interest amount on a sum of Rs. 2500 at 12% Compound Interest for 2 years?
   a) Rs. 325
   b) Rs. 636
   c) Rs. 450
   d) Rs. 500

23. A teacher buys a colour T.V. for Rs. 11256 at $8\frac{1}{3}$ % Compound Interest and repays the amount in 3 equal annual instalments, at the end of every year. How much should be paid in each instalment?
   a) Rs. 4100
   b) Rs. 4200
   c) Rs. 3800
   d) Rs. 4394

24. The marked price is 10% higher than the cost price. A discount of 10% is given on the marked price. In this kind of sale the seller has
   a) no loss, no gain
   b) looses
   c) gains
   d) lost 1%

25. A train goes at a speed of 54 kms per hour. It takes 15 seconds to cross a bridge of 150 m length. The length of the train is
   a) 50 m
   b) 75 m
   c) 60 m
   d) 80 m

• TEST No. 6 •

General Knowledge

1. The second largest State in India in population is
   a) Maharashtra
   b) Madhya Pradesh
   c) Andhra Pradesh
   d) Uttar Pradesh

2. The Rajya Sabha has a life of
   a) 6 years
   b) 2 years
   c) Permanency
   d) 7 years

3. The lower voting age in India is
   a) 18 years
   b) 21 years
   c) 27 years
   d) 24 years

4. The term of office of the Governor is
   a) 3 years
   b) 4 years
   c) 5 years
   d) 6 years

5. The famous king of the Kushana dynasty was
   a) Kuvishka
   b) Kanishka
   c) Pushya
   d) Kamarupa

6. The First President of India was
   a) Dr. V.V. Giri
   b) Dr. Zakir Hussain
   c) Dr. Rajendra Prasad
   d) Mr. Sanjiva Reddy

7. Kanchi was the capital of
   a) The Pallavas
   b) The Chalukyas
   c) The Rashtrakutas
   d) None of these

8. 'Kudavolai' system was in existence during the period of
   a) The Pallavas
   b) The Pandyas
   c) The Cholas
   d) None of these

9. The United Nations Organisation came into existence in
   a) 1920
   b) 1945
   c) 1935
   d) None of these

10. The emblem of UNO is
   a) Dove
   b) Apple
   c) Olive Branch
   d) None of these

11. Decimal coinage was introduced in India in the year
   a) 1850
   b) 1955
   c) 1957
   d) 1960

12. Full Moon occurs when
   a) Earth is between the Sun and the Moon
   b) Moon is between the Sun and the Earth
   c) Sun is between the Earth and the Moon
   d) None of these

13. Indian Standard Time (I.S.T.) is the local time of
   a) Delhi
   b) Allahabad
   c) Chennai
   d) Kolkata

14. The National Animal of India is
   a) Lion
   b) Tiger
   c) Elephant
   d) None of these

15. Shantivan is associated with
   a) Gandhi
   b) Nehru
   c) Lal Bahadur Sastri
   d) None of these

16. ICC's 2007, the World Cup Cricket was held in
    a) Kingston (West Indies)
    b) Kolkata (India)
    c) Sydney (Australia)
    d) Cape Town (S. Africa)

17. Viswanath Anand is associated with
    a) Volley Ball   b) Chess
    c) Carrom   d) None of these

18. 'Blood Circulation' was discovered by
    a) Alexander Fleming b) William Harvey
    c) Louis   d) None of these

19. 'Lactometer' is used to determine
    a) Hydrogen in water b) Purity of petrol
    c) Purity of milk   d) None of these

20. 'Radiator' is a
    a) Mixing agent   b) Cooling agent
    c) Separating agent d) None of these

21. A small gap is left between the joints of rails
    a) to produce sound
    b) to save the cost
    c) to accommodate expansion in summer
    d) None of these

22. 'Cataract' is a disease of
    a) Ears   b) Legs
    c) Eyes   d) None of these

23. When iron rusts, its weight
    a) Decreases   b) Increases
    c) Remains same   d) None of these

24. The largest gland in the human body is
    a) Pituitary   b) Adrenal
    c) Liver   d) None of these

25. The nearest planet to the Sun is
    a) Mercury   b) Pluto
    c) Jupiter   d) None of these

Reasoning - General Intelligence

1. Complete the series:
   1, 2, 3, 5, 8, 13 ......
   a) 34   b) 21
   c) 30   d) 35

2. Write the next number in the series: 14, 16, 13, 17, 12, 18, 11 .....
   a) 12   b) 19
   c) 22   d) 14

3. If $6 \times 2 = 31$, $8 \times 4 = 42$, $2 \times 2 = 11$, $6 \times 6 = 33$, then $8 \times 6 = ?$
   a) 33   b) 43
   c) 14   d) 42

4. Insert the missing number:

3	6	7
5	8	9
4	7	?

   a) 56   b) 13
   c) 8   d) 16

5. Insert the missing number:

8	5	3	10
7	6	6	7
14	8	9	?

   a) 17   b) 72
   c) 16   d) 13

6. Find the number in the series:
   0, 6, 24, 60, 120, 210, ...
   a) 420   b) 336
   c) 504   d) 1

7. Insert the number missing from brackets:
   188   (300)   263
   893   (   )   915
   a) 150   b) 44
   c) 88   d) 96

8. Find the next number in the series:
   $2, 1, \dfrac{1}{3}, \dfrac{2}{3}, 0$?
   a) 1   b) $-\dfrac{2}{3}$
   c) $1\dfrac{1}{2}$ d) $\dfrac{2}{3}$

9. Of the following the one that is not equivalent to 376 is:
   a) $(2 \times 100) + (17 \times 10) + 6$
   b) $(3 \times 100) + (7 \times 10) + 6$
   c) $(2 \times 106) + (16 \times 10) + 106$
   d) $(2 \times 100) + (7 \times 10) + 106$

Directions (Qns. 10-11): Find the correct alternative in each case

10. 0, 6, 24, 60, 120, ?
    a) 160   b) 156
    c) 210   d) 180

11. 11, 24, 67, 122, 219, ?
    a) 300   b) 325
    c) 316   d) 340

12. One third of A's marks in Arithmetic, equals to half of his marks in English. If he gets 150 marks in the two subjects together, how many marks has he got in English?
    a) 60   b) 120
    c) 180   d) 30

13. In a row of children, Shirish is 7th from the left and Charu is 4th from right. When Shirish and Charu exchange positions, Shirish will be 13th from the left. Which will be Charu's position from the right?
    a) 4th
    b) 8th
    c) 11th
    d) 10th

14. Four of the following numbers are alike in some way. Which one is not?
    19, 29, 21, 23, 13
    a) 23   b) 21
    c) 13   d) 29

15. $\dfrac{16 \times 17}{(57 + 79)4} =$
    a) 0.50   b) 0.72
    c) 1.9   d) 8.0

Directions (Qns. 16-18): Insert the missing number

16. 9   4   32
    15 5   70
    17 3   ?
    a) 14   b) 64
    c) 51   d) 48

17. 8   3   21
    6   5   25
    12 2   ?
    a) 22   b) 76
    c) 19   d) 196

18. 4   6   3   8
    2   8   4   4
    6   5   ?   10
    a) 4   b) 3
    c) 8   d) 9

19. How many 8's are there in the following sequence, which are preceded by 5, but not immediately followed by 3?
    5 8 3 7 5 8 6 3 8 5 4 5 8 4
    7 6 5 5 8 3 5 8 7 5 8 2 8 5
    a) 0   b) 1
    c) 2   d) 4

20. 45 per cent of a number is 1089. The number is
    a) 2420   b) 5384
    c) 6310   d) 2240

21. A tap can fill a tank in 2 hours and by another tap, the tank becomes empty in 3 hours. In how much time will the tank be full when both the taps are open?
    a) 1½ hrs.   b) 2½ hrs.
    c) 4 hrs.   d) 6 hrs.

22. I bought one dozen pencils at the rate of 5 paise per pencil. For how much should one pencil be sold for a profit of 20%?
    a) 5 paise   b) 6 paise
    c) 7 paise   d) 10 paise

23. Sixteen men can complete a piece of work in 25 days. In how many days can 20 men complete that piece of work?
    a) 20 days   b) 22 days
    c) 18 days   d) 16 days

24. 200 ÷ 20 ÷ 100 = ?
    a) 6   b) 10
    c) 0.1   d) 1000

Direction (Qn. 25): In this question there is a question mark in blank space in which only one of the four alternatives given under the question satisfies the same relationship as is found between two terms on the left of sign (::) given in the question.

25. 12 : 30 :: 56 : ?
    a) 120   b) 140
    c) 72   d) 64

General English

Directions (Qns. 1-4): Mark the part which has grammatical mistake.

1. He is a / man whom / I know / is trustworthy.
       a   (b)   c   d

2. I / bathe / myself / every day.
     a   b   (c)   d

3. You are / speaking a / white lie.
       a   (b)   c

4. No one got a / prize except / I.
        a   b   (c)

Directions (Qns. 5-6): Select a word or phrase from the given list to complete the sentences.

5. With what colour are you going to have your house painted? We will _____
   a) paint it white
   b) paint white
   c) have painted it white
   d) have it painted white

6. Does your father know _____ in English?
   a) that why you failed
   b) why you failed
   c) did you fail
   d) why have you been failed

Directions (Qns. 7-9): Supply suitable prepositions from the given ones (where needed) in the blank spaces in the following sentences.

7. I am fed up _____ staying at this place.
   a) at   b) on
   c) for   (d) with

8. I was delighted _____ his unexpected arrival.
   a) at   (b) for
   c) of   d) in

9. I prefer coffee _____ tea.
   a) on   (b) than
   c) any   (d) to

Directions (Qns. 10-11): Collective nouns : Pick out the correct nouns from the words given :

10. The hunter had a _____ of arrows in his quiver.

a) bunch   b) set
c) sheaf   d) faggot

11. The artist arranged an exhibition of a _____ of his pictures.
    a) flight   b) group
    c) gallery   d) parade

Directions (Qns. 12-13): Mark the correct meaning:

12. **anonymous**
    a) generous
    b) stingy
    c) well-known
    d) one whose name is not known

13. **atheist**
    a) believer in religion
    b) disbeliever in God
    c) priest
    d) bachelor

Directions (Qns. 14-17): Choose the word or phrase which is opposite in meaning to the key word.

14. **Native**
    a) alien   c) innate
    c) aboriginal d) fragile

15. **Neglect**
    a) care   b) oversight
    c) renovate d) quantify

16. **Scold**
    a) berate   b) vituperate
    c) loyal   d) praise

17. **Severe**
    a) relentless b) intense
    c) lenient   d) unadorned

Directions (Qns. 18-20): In the words given below if the spelling is correct, put 'C', if wrong put 'W'.

18. sucess

19. absence

20. superintendant   *unamed*

*Directions (Qns. 21-22): Each of the following sentences has a word or words in **italics**. Replace them by the verb indicated against each sentence without changing the meaning.*

21. As soon as he entered the hall he *went straight to* the dining table (Make)

22. You must *find the meaning of* the word in your dictionary (Look)

Directions (Qns. 23-25): Change the following sentences into 'indirect speech.'

23. Her mother told her, "Beauty does not need any ornament".

24. He told his mother, "She is unfit for her job".

25. He asked, "Shall I sit down in this place for a few minutes".

Arithmetic - Numerical Ability

1. A sum at Simple Interest amounts to Rs. 1000 in 2 yrs and Rs. 4000 in 5 yrs. Find the sum and rate of interest.
   a) 1300   b) 1400
   c) 1200   d) 1500

2. The difference between the Simple Interest and Compound Interest on a certain sum for 2 years at 15% interest is Rs.90. Find the Principal.
   a) 3000   b) 3500
   c) 4000   d) 2500

3. A 100 m long train crosses a stationary man in 10 seconds. What is the speed of the train?
   a) 35   b) 36
   c) 70   d) 72

4. By selling 15 pencils for Rs. 30, Rahim lost 20%. How many should he sell for Rs. 52 to have a gain of 30%?
   a) 40   b) 16
   c) 35   d) 50

5. Convert 0.05 into percentage
   Hint : Percentages are expressed as a fraction of 100.
   a) 5%   b) .05%
   c) 50%   d) $\frac{1}{2}$%

6. What percent of $\frac{5}{8}$ is $\frac{8}{5}$?
   a) 128   b) 256
   c) 8   d) 5

7. A number when divided by 3, is reduced by 20. The number is
   a) 33   b) 30
   c) 21   d) 60

8. Three-fourth of a certain number is 60. Half of that number is
   a) 20   b) 30
   c) 40   d) 80

9. The difference of two numbers is 11 and 1/3 of their sum is 7. Then one number is
   a) 16   b) 11
   c) 7   d) 10

10. Three numbers are in the ratio 3 : 4 : 5 and their average is 24. The largest number is
    a) 10   b) 15
    c) 45   d) 30

11. If a : b = 2 : 3 and b : c = 3 : 4. Find a : b : c and a : c.
    a) 1:2   b) 2:1
    c) 1:3   d) 3:1

12. If A : B = 3 : 4, B : C = 4 : 5 and C : D = 6 : 7, A : D = ?
    a) $\frac{35}{18}$ b) $\frac{18}{35}$
    c) $\frac{5}{7}$ d) $\frac{6}{7}$

13. Find the area of a triangle whose sides measures 15 cm, 16 cm, 17cm.
    a) 110   b) 109.98
    c) 112   d) 111

14. Find the HCF of $\frac{6}{8}$, $2\frac{1}{2}$ and $\frac{15}{16}$
    a) $\frac{5}{16}$ b) $\frac{8}{16}$
    c) $\frac{1}{16}$ d) $\frac{10}{16}$

15. Simplify:

$$1\frac{1}{7} \text{ of } 3\frac{1}{2} - \frac{4}{15} \text{ of } 3\frac{3}{4}$$

    a) 7   b) 3

    c) 1   d) 4

16. Find the square root of 0.000943

    a) 0.30   b) 0.3030708

    c) 0.03037   d) 0.308

17. $\sqrt{10}$ = 3.162, $\sqrt{5}$ = 2.236. Find $\dfrac{\sqrt{10} - \sqrt{5}}{\sqrt{2}}$

    a) 0.65   b) 0.056

    c) 0.655   d) 0.565

18. The average age of a class of 22 students is 21 years. The average increases by 1 when the teacher's age is also included. What is the age of the teacher?

    a) 44   b) 43

    c) 41   d) 40

19. A : B = 2 : 3, C : B = 3 : 4. Then A : C =

    a) 2:3   b) 2:4

    c) 8:9   d) 9:8

20. A and B can do a piece of work in 45 and 40 days respectively. After some days A leaves. B finished the work in 23 days. After how many days did A leave?

    a) 6   b) 8

    c) 9   d) 10

21. What is the square root of 0.09?

    a) 0.3   b) 0.03

    c) 0.003   d) 3.0

Directions (Qns. 22-25): Find the value of question mark (?) in each question.

22. 250 × 350 − 170 = ?

    a) 14400   b) 28000

    c) 45000   d) 87330

23. $7\dfrac{1}{2} + 6\dfrac{2}{5} - 3\dfrac{1}{4} = ?$

    a) $10\dfrac{13}{20}$ b) $10\dfrac{3}{5}$

    c) $11\dfrac{13}{20}$ d) $16\dfrac{13}{20}$

24. 5.6 × 4.5 + 3.4 = ?

    a) 123.24   b) 73.6

    c) 57.54   d) None of these

25. 40.84 × 5.5 + 4.5 × 6.40 = ?

    a) 253.42   b) 2613.76

    c) 243.12   d) 1400.812

◦ TEST No. 7 ◦

General Knowledge

1. The difference between Greenwich Mean Time and Indian Standard Time is

    a) 12 hours   b) 6½ hours

    c) 6 hours   d) 5½ hours

2. Savannas are

    a) Tropical grass lands

    b) Tracts full of trees

    c) Vast plains   d) Mountains

3. Fauna is

    a) animal life of a region

    b) plant life of a region

    c) study of Oceanography

    d) study of Physics

4. Alluvial soil is formed by deposits brought by

    a) Rivers   b) Sea

    c) Small streams   d) Channels

5. The farthest planet to Sun is

    a) Mars   b) Neptune

    c) Pluto   d) Venus

6. Bauxite is an ore of

    a) Iron   b) Lead

    c) Aluminium   d) None of these

7. The capital of Uttar Pradesh is

    a) Kanpur   b) Lucknow

    c) Allahabad   d) Meerut

8. 'Land of Rising Sun' is called
   a) Vietnam   b) Australia
   c) Japan   d) None of these

9. The former name of 'Reserve Bank of India' was
   a) Imperial Bank of India
   b) National Bank of India
   c) Central Bank of India
   d) None of these

10. Silver is mostly found in
    a) Karnataka   b) Madhya Pradesh
    c) Tamil Nadu   d) None of these

11. Tri-colour is the name of the flag of
    a) United Kingdom   b) India
    c) United States of America
    d) None of these

12. Lumbini is associated with
    a) Lord Buddha   b) Mahavira
    c) Napoleon   d) None of these

13. The term 'nautical mile' is used in
    a) Ships   b) Aeroplanes
    c) Cars   d) None of these

14. Jesus Christ was born in
    a) Tel-Aviv   b) Jerusalem
    c) Bethelehem   d) None of these

15. The currency of Bangladesh is
    a) Taka   b) Kata
    c) Rupee   d) None of these

16. The term 'Chinaman' is associated with
    a) Football   b) Cricket
    c) Swimming   d) None of these

17. 'Wankhede Stadium' is at
    a) Chennai   b) Kolkata
    c) Mumbai   d) None of these

18. Who is the Author of the book *"India 2020"*?
    a) R.K. Narayan
    b) Dr. A.P.J. Abdul Kalam
    c) Sidney Shelton   d) Nibal Singh

19. The 'Solar System' was discovered by
    a) Galleleo   b) Copernicus
    c) Finsen   d) None of these

20. 'Seismograph' is used to record
    a) Earthquakes   b) Heart beats
    c) The speed of military aircrafts
    d) None of these

21. 'Philately' deals with
    a) Coin collection b) Stamp collection
    c) Stone collection d) None of these

22. The sea-water is saline because
    a) The sea-weeds emit salts
    b) The rivers bring salts
    c) The rain brings salts
    d) None of these

23. 'Diphtheria' affects
    a) Throat   b) Lungs
    c) Ears   d) None of these

24. Green plants store their food in
    a) Stems   b) Leaves
    c) Roots   d) None of these

25. How many planets are there in the Solar System?
    a) 8   b) 12
    c) 10   d) 9

Reasoning - General Intelligence

1. Usha is twice as old as Rita. Three years ago she was three times as old as Rita. How old is Usha now?
   a) 7 years   b) 9 years
   c) 6 years   d) 12 years

2. Supply the missing figure:
   2, 6, 12, 20, 30 56
   a) 42   b) 38
   c) 46   d) 56

3. If HKUJ means FISH, what does UVCD mean?
   a) STAR   b) STAK
   c) STAL   d) STAB

4. If 2=5, 4=18, 6=39, 8=68, then 10 = ?
   a) 54   b) 105
   c) 81   d) 95

5. If A=2, B=3, C=4 and so on, what does the following number stand for 14, 2, 11, 16, 19 ?
   a) NBKNS   b) KLEVE
   c) MAJOR   d) TEACH

Find the next number in the series (2 questions given below)

6. 24, 72, 36, 108, 54, 162, ...
   a) 63
   b) 227
   c) 243
   d) 81

7. 8, 0, 15, 9, 22, 18, 29, 27, ...
   a) 63
   b) 127
   c) 243
   d) 36

8. When   8 × 3 = 26
            16 × 5 = 82
   then   32 × 2 = ?
   a) 99
   b) 66
   c) 120
   d) 90

9. What per cent is 14 of 23?
   a) 60%
   b) $61\frac{1}{2}\%$
   c) $60\frac{20}{23}\%$
   d) $60\frac{1}{3}\%$

Directions (Qns. 10-11): In each of the following questions select the similar pair as related to that given in the question.

10. Fibre : Fabric : :
    a) average : aggregate
    b) nucleus : cell
    c) member : league
    d) subject : object

11. Skeleton : Body : :
    a) Prisoner : cell
    b) Law : society
    c) Prisoner : law
    d) Jury : sentence

Find the next alternative:

12. $-\frac{1}{2}, -\frac{1}{6}, \frac{1}{6}, \frac{1}{2}, \frac{5}{6}$
    a) $1\frac{1}{2}$
    b) $2\frac{1}{2}$
    c) $1\frac{1}{3}$
    d) $1\frac{1}{6}$

Rearrange the letter to make a meaningful word in the questions (13-15) and do as directed:

13. BEDAISET (a disease)
    Find the last alphabet of the rearranged word:
    a) O
    b) E
    c) S
    d) B

14. ECLLOEG
    Write the middle alphabet of the rearranged word:

   a) L
   b) O
   c) C
   d) K

15. DYEPROJA
    Find the last letter (alphabet) of the rearranged word.
    a) P
    b) O
    c) Y
    d) A

16. 20 men can dig 40 holes in 60 days. If so, 10 men can dig 20 holes in how many days?
    a) 30 days
    b) 45 days
    c) 60 days
    d) 75 days

17. Antony is to Cleopatra as Krishna is to ......
    a) Sassi
    b) Punnu
    c) Radha
    d) Ranja

18. Mark the odd place:
    a) Venice
    b) London
    c) Paris
    d) Madrid

19. For a given perimeter which has the maximum area
    a) square
    b) circle
    c) rectangle
    d) heptagon

20. Mark the odd place:
    a) Canada
    b) Australia
    c) New Zealand
    d) United States

21. Collect is to Distribute as Earn is to ....
    a) store
    b) bank
    c) enjoy
    d) spend

The following series are in order. One number/ letter is to be filled up by you. Four alternate answers have been suggested. Mark the correct one.

22. a, e, j, o, t, y
    a) d
    b) z
    c) e
    d) n

23. 1, 5, 11, 19, 29, ..., 55
    a) 42
    b) 41
    c) 40
    d) 32

24. 6, 7, 18, 23, 38, ...
    a) 49
    b) 47
    c) 87
    d) 92

25. 6, 30, 260, 3130, ...
    a) 5782
    b) 56442
    c) 107662
    d) 46662

General English

Mark the part which has grammatical mistake:

1. Being a / cold day I / did not go /
   (a)   (b)   (c)
   out of my room.
            (d)

2. One / should do / his duty / honestly.
   (a)   (b)   (c)   (d)

3. He is / best boy / of his / class.
   (a)   (b)   (c)   (d)

Choose the correct word or phrase:

4. He was _____ of all his valuable possession.
   a) stolen   b) robbed
   c) pinched   d) theft

5. Salt _____ in water but was doesn't.
   a) melts   b) drowns
   c) dissolves   d) immerses

6. Charles' marriage _____ Diana was much talked about.
   a) to   b) with
   c) between   d) of

7. The insects are a great nuisance _____ us.
   a) with   b) for
   c) to   d) upon

(Vocabulary) Mark the correct meaning:

8. **Stamp collector**
   a) Phillanderer   b) Bibliographer
   c) Philatelist   d) None of these

9. **lenient**
   a) tall   b) not strict
   c) wise   d) lean

10. **warrant**
    a) to justify   b) argue
    c) arrest   d) long for

11. **commit**
    a) to add up   b) to prove
    c) to entrust   d) to urge

Mark the correct antonym of:

12. **authentic**
    a) real   b) authoritative
    c) false   d) inattentive

13. **deficit**
    a) enough   b) less
    c) surplus   d) more

14. **vulgar**
    a) ugly   b) decent
    c) indecent   d) smooth

15. **entry**
    a) way out   b) admission
    c) exit   d) outpass

In the words given below if the spelling is correct, put 'C', if wrong, put 'W'

16. **receive**

17. **preseverence**

Choose (a) or (b) whichever is right in spelling:

18. a) liesure   b) leisure

19. a) concreet   b) concrete

Fill up the blanks with correct words:

20. **A drowning man will catch _____**
    a) another drowning man
    b) a life boat
    c) a rock
    d) a straw

21. **God helps those who help _____**
    a) others   b) the poor
    c) the needy   d) themselves

22. **Necessity is the _____ of invention.**
    a) mother   b) father
    c) daughter   d) cause

Choose the most idiomatic and appropriate word/phrase:

23. **Some people want to become rich by _____**
    a) all means   b) hook or crook
    c) no means   d) hard work

24. **Once there lived a man _____ name Rip van Winkle.**
    a) with   b) of
    c) by   d) whose

25. **A judge should be _____ in a case he is trying.**
    a) Impartial   b) Uninterested
    c) Concerned   d) Zealous

Arithmetic - Numerical Ability

1. The average of 5 numbers is 6; The average of 3 numbers is 4; what is the average of remaining two numbers?
   a) 9
   b) 21
   c) 12
   d) 8

2. At simple interest a sum of money is doubled in 20 years. What is the rate of interest?
   a) 20
   b) 4
   c) 5
   d) 10

3. The compound interest on Rs.3000 for 3 years at 10% per annum is
   a) Rs. 900
   b) Rs. 933
   c) Rs. 963
   d) Rs. 993

4. A, B and C can do a piece of work in 7 days, 14 days and 28 days respectively. If they work together, the work will be finished in
   a) 2 days
   b) 3 days
   c) 4 days
   d) 5 days

5. The diameter of a cone is 1.4 cm. Its slant height is 4.2 cm. Find the curved surface area.
   a) 9.24 cm^2
   b) 2.24 cm^2
   c) 8.14 cm^2
   d) 6.94 cm^2

6. Find the value of
   $12 \times 12 + 2 \times 12 \times 15 + 15 \times 15$.
   a) 729
   b) 749
   c) 725
   d) 745

7. What is the ratio of 1m 50 cm to 1m 80 cm?
   a) 5 : 6
   b) 4 : 5
   c) 2 : 3
   d) 3 : 4

8. Find the LCM of 50 and 40.
   a) 5
   b) 200
   c) 4
   d) 100

9. In a triangle of XYZ, XY the adjacent side is 5 cm; the opposite side YZ is 6 cm and the hypotenuse ZX is 8 cm. Then find tan of X.

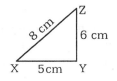

a) $\dfrac{6}{5}$
b) $\dfrac{5}{6}$
c) $\dfrac{5}{8}$
d) $\dfrac{8}{5}$

10. What decimal fraction of a Kg is 510 gms?
    a) 5.1
    b) 0.051
    c) 0.51
    d) 0.0051

11. Which is the greatest fraction?
    a) 7/8
    b) 6/7
    c) 8/10
    d) 8/9

12. A train 150 m long crossed 175 m long platform in 13 seconds. Calculate the speed of the train in km/hr.
    a) 90
    b) 100
    c) 110
    d) 150

13. If A : B = 2 : 3 , B : C = 4 : 5, C : D = 6 : 7, A : D = ?
    a) 2 : 7
    b) 7 : 8
    c) 16 : 35
    d) 4 : 13

14. The equal value of 56 meters is
    a) 560 hm.
    b) 0.56 cm.
    c) 5.6 deca m.
    d) 5.6 m

15. Which ratio is greater?
    a) 12 Km : 30 Km
    b) 15 litres : 65 litres
    c) 20 litres : 45 litres
    d) 10 Rs : 10 Ps.

16. $\left(\dfrac{5}{6} + \dfrac{11}{16}\right) \div \dfrac{73}{24} = ?$

    a) $\dfrac{1}{4}$
    b) $\dfrac{73}{24}$
    c) $\dfrac{1}{2}$
    d) $\dfrac{1}{3}$

17. $1 + \cfrac{1}{1 + \cfrac{1}{1 - \cfrac{1}{6}}} = ?$

    a) $\dfrac{6}{11}$
    b) $\dfrac{7}{6}$
    c) $\dfrac{1}{6}$
    d) $\dfrac{16}{11}$

18. $4\frac{2}{3} \times 3\frac{1}{5} + 1\frac{1}{2} = $?

   a) $5\frac{1}{3}$ b) $5\frac{1}{5}$

   c) $8\frac{1}{5}$ d) None of these

19. In the following number series a wrong number is given; find out that wrong number?

   14.5, 15.5, 17.5, 20, 24.5, 29.5

   a) 15.5   b) 20

   c) 17.5   d) 24.5

20. 30% of 1860 + 40% of 820 = ? % of 3544

   a) 30   b) 25

   c) 35   d) 40

21. A 140 metres long train crosses a signal post in 7 seconds. What is the speed of the train in kmph?

   a) 72   b) 64

   c) 84   d) Data inadequate

22. The price of four dozens of pens is Rs. 748.8 What will be the approximate price of 2 such pens?

   a) Rs. 450   b) Rs. 500

   c) Rs. 475   d) Rs. 425

23. $\frac{19}{7} \times \frac{64}{18} \times \frac{21}{38} \times \frac{54}{16} = $?

   a) 9   b) 18

   c) $\frac{1}{2}$ d) $\frac{32}{21}$

24. 999 + 99 + 9999 = ?

   a) 11087

   b) 9997

   c) 11098

   d) None of these

25. What should be added to 18962 to mak it exactly divisible by 13?

   a) 1   b) 2

   c) 5   d) 4

TEST No. 8

General Knowledge

1. Nilgiri Hills are known as
   a) Roof of the World   b) Tea Treasures
   c) Blue Mountains   d) None of these

2. STD is the abbreviation for
   a) Subscribers Trunk Dialing
   b) Software Technology Department
   c) Staff Training Division
   d) None of these

3. Sriharikota is famous for
   a) Satellite launching
   b) Thermal Power station
   c) Air base
   d) None of these

4. 'The Tripitaka' is the sacred text of
   a) Shintoism   b) Buddhism
   c) Hinduism   d) None of these

5. 'Mecca' is a sacred place for
   a) Buddhists   b) Christians
   c) Muslims
   d) None of these

6. 'The Leaning Tower' is located in
   a) Germany   b) Italy
   c) France   d) London

7. The epic 'Periya Puranam' was written by
   a) Sekkizhar   b) Pugazhendhi
   c) Paranjothi Munivar d) Ramanujar

8. 'Mount Everest' is located in
   a) India   b) Nepal
   c) China   d) None of these

9. Name the first Indian Nobel Prize winner
   a) Rabindranath Tagore
   b) Amartya Sen
   c) Mother Teresa
   d) None of these

10. The microscope is used to study
   a) Distant objects   b) Nearby objects
   c) Small objects   d) None of these

11. Wright Brothers are associated with
   a) Balloon   b) Bicycle
   c) Aeroplane   d) None of these

12. The highest mountain peak in Tamil Nadu is
    a) Perumalmalai
    b) Dottabetta
    c) Thiruneermalai
    d) Nilgiris

13. *'Gitanjali'* was written by
    a) Jawaharlal Nehru
    b) Rabindranath Tagore
    c) V.S. Naipaul
    d) Mrinalini

14. E-mail means
    a) electronic mail
    b) economic mail
    c) easy mail
    d) None of these

15. The number of official languages in our country is
    a) 12
    b) 16
    c) 22
    d) 18

16. X-rays were discovered by
    a) J.J. Thomson
    b) James Chadwick
    c) Roentgen
    d) None of these

17. The Atomic power reactor is located in Tamil Nadu at
    a) Neyveli
    b) Kalpakkam
    c) Mettur
    d) Kayankulam

18. The unit of power is
    a) joule
    b) watt
    c) newton
    d) volt

19. In plants, roots develop from
    a) Plumule
    b) Ligule
    c) Radicle
    d) None of these

20. Name the Indian leader who was given the title of 'Lokmanya' by the people during freedom struggle
    a) Lala Lajapat Rai
    b) Bal Gangadhara Tilak
    c) Aurobindo Ghosh
    d) None of these

21. The last Viceroy of British India was
    a) Lord Wavel
    b) Lord Mountbatten
    c) Sir Stafford Cripps
    d) None of these

22. The famous Siva temple at Thanjavur was built by
    a) Raja Raja Chola
    b) Karikal Chola
    c) Mahendra Chola
    d) Rajendra Chola

23. Rice and Wheat are
    a) Millets
    b) Pulses
    c) Cereals
    d) None of these

24. Coffee is cultivated mostly in the States of
    a) Karnataka & Andhra Pradesh
    b) Kerala & Karnataka
    c) Kerala & Tamil Nadu
    d) None of these

25. The reservoir behind 'Mettur Dam' is known as
    a) Stanley Reservoir
    b) Mettur Reservoir
    c) Cauvery Reservoir
    d) None of these

Reasoning - General Intelligence

Directions (Qns. 1 & 2): In each of the following questions what should come in the place of question-mark (?) in the given number series?

1. 6, 7, 14, 69, ?
    a) 174
    b) 450
    c) 630
    d) 70

2. 2, 6, 12, 20, 30, 42, ?
    a) 53
    b) 54
    c) 55
    d) 56

3. If 'A' means '×', 'B' means '−', 'C' means '÷' and 'D' means '+', then what will be the value of the following expression?
    50B 10D3 A25 C5
    a) 25
    b) 105
    c) 215
    d) 55

4. How many 4s are there in the following number series which are immediately preceded by 5 and immediately followed by 6?
    7 8 3 2 1 4 5 6 2 5 4 6 7 6 3 2 5 4 6 8 5 4 3 7 5 4 6
    a) One
    b) Two
    c) Three
    d) Four

Directions (Qns. 5 & 6): In each of the following questions select the similar pair as related to that given in the question.

5. Sailor : Ship :: ?
    a) Clerk : Site
    b) Teacher : College
    c) Beautician : Stage
    d) Pilot : Cockpit

6. Author : Pen :: ?
    a) Chef : Knife
    b) Mason : Chisel
    c) Surgeon : Anvil
    d) Blacksmith : Saw

7. In a certain code language **SUN** is written as 579 and **MORTAL** is written as 364120. How the word **TATA SUMO** be written in that code of language?
   a) 12127536
   b) 12126573
   c) 12125763
   d) 12125736

8. In a row of girls, if Latha who is 10th from the left and Vijaya who is 9th from the right interchange their positions, Latha becomes 15th from the left. How many girls are there in the row?
   a) 23
   b) 16
   c) 19
   d) 18

9. In a certain code language **LADY** is written as 5183 and **PERSON** is written as 962704. How would the word **PLAYER** be written in that code language?
   a) 951362
   b) 968352
   c) 915263
   d) Data inadequate

Directions (Qns. 10-11): Find the odd one out from the given alternatives.

10. a) Cock
    b) Eagle
    c) Parrot
    d) Crow

11. a) Stream
    b) Lake
    c) Brook
    d) River

Directions (Qns. 12-13): Which answer figure will complete the question figure?

12. Question Figure   Answer Figure

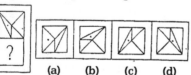
(a) (b) (c) (d)

13. Question Figure   Answer Figure

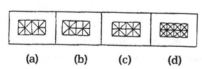
(a) (b) (c) (d)

Directions (Qns. 14-15): Which one of the given responses would be a meaningful order of the following words?

14. 1. Rock   2. Hill   3. Mountain
    4. Range   5. Stone

a) 5, 1, 2, 3, 4
b) 4, 3, 2, 5, 1
c) 5, 2, 3 4, 1
d) 1, 2, 3, 4, 5

15. 1. Sapling   2. Seed   3. Tree
    4. Plant   5. Branches

a) 2, 1, 4, 3, 5
b) 1, 2, 3, 4, 5
c) 4, 2, 1, 3, 5
d) 5, 3, 2, 1, 4

Directions (Qns. 16-17): Find the related word/ letters/numbers/figure to complete the Analogy.

16. 13 : 93 :: 17 : ?
    a) 39
    b) 15
    c) 51
    d) 31

17. 256 : 12 :: 225 : ?
    a) 13
    b) 9
    c) 11
    d) 10

Directions (Qns. 18-20): In each of the following questions what should come in the place of question Mark?

18.
    15 △ 9   3 △ 22   6 △ 7
      23   92   ?
      8   4   30

    a) 40
    b) 43
    c) 34
    d) 100

19.

15	6	5
13	3	9
8	2	?
20	7	13

a) 4
b) 7
c) 6
d) 1

20.
    (65|13 / 18|9)   (85|17 / 24|12)   (55|? / 28|14)

    a) 12
    b) 11
    c) 28
    d) 10

Directions (Qns. 21-22): In each of the following questions select the set which is most like the given set.

21. Given set: [9, 36, 54]
    a) [10, 40, 50]
    b) [12, 48, 72]
    c) [8, 40, 48]
    d) [11, 44, 77]

22. Given set: [5, 30, 120]
    a) [7, 56, 325]
    b) [6, 40, 212]
    c) [3, 12, 24]
    d) [4, 22, 60]

Directions (Qns. 23-25): In each question below, there are certain words. You have to arrange each word in a meaningful order.

23. 1. Andhra Pradesh   2. Universe
    3. Tirupati   4. World
    5. India
    a) 54213
    b) 21354
    c) 15324
    d) 31542

24. 1. Errata   2. Subject matter
    3. Heading   4. Chapter
    5. Introduction
    a) 51423   b) 32514
    c) 32541   d) 23451

25. 1. Consultation   2. Disease
    3. Doctor   4. Treatment
    5. Recovery
    a) 23415   b) 23145
    c) 51432   d) 43125

General English

Directions (Qns. 1-3): Mark the part which has grammatical mistake.

1. Though he / is poor / but he / is honest.
       (a)   (b)   (c)   (d)
2. You must / listen / what I / say.
       (a)   (b)   (c)   (d)
3. This man/is senior/than that man/in service.
       (a)   (b)   (c)   (d)

Directions (Qns. 4-5): Choose the correct word or phrase.

4. He talked so softly that nobody could .... what he said.
   a) listen to   b) hear
   c) hear to   d) none of these
5. He was .... my hand so tightly that I could not pull it away.
   a) catching   b) holding
   c) seizing   d) none of these

Directions (Qns. 6-7): Choose the most appropriate word from the set of words given under each sentence to fill the blank.

6. It was difficult to see through the _____ of the headlights.
   a) shine   b) glare
   c) dazzle   d) none of these
7. Children enjoy _____ coloured water at each other on the occasion of the Holi.
   a) squirting
   b) pouring
   c) spilling
   d) none of these

Directions (Qns. 8-9): Mark the correct meaning:

8. **magnanimous**
   a) puzzling   b) generous
   c) foolish   d) unnecessary
9. **warrant**
   a) to justify   b) argue
   c) arrest   d) long for

Directions (Qns. 10-12): Against each key word are given four suggested meanings. Choose the word or phrase which is OPPOSITE in meaning to the key word.

10. **Terrible**
    a) delightful   b) hideous
    c) devout   d) fortunate
11. **Ugly**
    a) repellent   b) uncomely
    c) attractive   d) clever
12. **Nasty**
    a) loathsome   b) clean
    c) starry   d) renowned

Directions (Qns. 13-15): Tick only the misspelled word or words in each group.

13. a) privilege   b) separate
    c) incidentally   d) occurence
14. a) precede   b) exceed
    c) accede   d) procede
15. a) pronunciation
    b) noticable
    c) desirable
    d) holiday

Directions (Qns. 16-18): *Fill in the blanks with the right word in each case. The right word should be connected with the word in ITALICS in the first sentence of each pair. Write the correct word.*

EXAMPLES :   He and his friends *agreed.*

He and his friends made an

_____

ANSWER : Agreement

16. The director *decided* that John should go.

It was the .... of the director that John should go.

17. He *knew* chemistry very well.

He had a good .... of chemistry.

18. The electric supply was *discontinued* (cut)

Directions (Qns. 19-20): *Write out the following sentences using the most appropriate tense or form of the verbs in brackets. The words in brackets should be put in their correct position in relation to the verb:*

19. Come in now. I am sorry (keep) you waiting.

20. If you (buy) a car today, it (cost) you a lot of money.

Directions (Qns. 21-23): *Select the correct form of the pronoun in the following sentences from the alternatives given.*

21. It is for .... young people to be architects of the future. (we, us)

22. With .... are you travelling? (who, whom)

23. "Whose book is this?". "It is ...." (our, ours)

Directions (Qns. 24-25): *Change the following sentences into indirect speech.*

24. The teacher said to Chathurvedi, "If you do not listen to what I say, you will be punished".

25. The teacher said to the boys, "You shall complete one exercise before the end of the hour".

Arithmetic - Numerical Ability

1.
```
        5 6
    7 4 * 1
          8
  +   9 4 6
  ─────────
    8 4 3 1
```
a) 5   b) 2
c) 7   d) 8

2.
```
      * * *
    9 9 9 9
  + 9 0 0 6
  ─────────
    2 0 0 0
```
a) 985   b) 915
c) 955   d) None of these

3. $\sqrt{\dfrac{4}{5} \times \dfrac{9}{125}}$

a) $\dfrac{18}{25}$ b) $\dfrac{12}{125}$

c) $\dfrac{6}{25}$ d) 0.316

4. A certain sum of money amounts to Rs.770/- in one year and amounts to Rs.847 in two years at certain rate of interest. Find the sum.
a) Rs.700   b) Rs.600
c) Rs.500   d) Rs.400

5. $1\dfrac{1}{3} \times 3\dfrac{7}{8} \div 1\dfrac{3}{5} =$

a) $\dfrac{155}{64}$ b) $\dfrac{48}{155}$

c) $\dfrac{155}{48}$ d) $\dfrac{155}{24}$

6. Express 12.5 percent as a fraction

a) $\dfrac{1}{4}$ b) $\dfrac{1}{8}$

c) $\dfrac{1}{16}$ d) $\dfrac{1}{32}$

7. A earns 10% more than B, but 15% less than C. If B earns Rs.85/-, then C earns
a) Rs. 110/-   b) Rs. 105/-
c) Rs. 25/-   d) Rs. 115/-

8. If Rs. 91/- is divided among A, B, C in the ratio $1\frac{1}{2} : 3\frac{2}{3} : 2\frac{3}{4}$, B will get
   a) Rs. 36
   b) Rs. 40
   c) Rs. 45
   d) Rs. 48

9. A radio dealer fixed the Selling Price of a transistor radio at Rs.144 each at a profit of 12½%. 3 transistors broke into pieces and rest were sold at the fixed Selling Price. If his loss on the whole was Rs.96, how many transistors did he have in the beginning?
   a) 18
   b) 21
   c) 15
   d) 12

10. $63 \div \sqrt{0.0049}$
    a) 1.285
    b) 900
    c) 90
    d) 12.85

11. A bag contains a number of 10 paise, 20 paise, 25 paise coins in the ratio of 7:4:3. If the money value comes to be Rs.90/-, the number of 25 paise coins in the bag is
    a) 120
    b) 160
    c) 280
    d) 30

12. 'A' does work in 5 days for which 'B' takes only 4 days. 'C' does a work in 3 days for which B takes only 2 days. If Rs. 7.40 be the daily wage for their combined work, then A's share will be
    a) Rs. 3
    b) Rs. 2.40
    c) Rs. 2
    d) Rs. 1.50

13. The total salary of 2 watchmen is Rs.510. One spends 80% of his salary and the other 70%. If their savings are in ratio 3:4, what are their salaries?
    a) Rs.200 & Rs.250
    b) Rs.280 & Rs.220
    c) Rs.300 & Rs.200
    d) Rs.270 & Rs.240

14. There are 5 numbers. The average of first four is 8 and the last four is 10. If the first number is 4, what is the last number?
    a) 20
    b) 18
    c) 12
    d) 10

15. The value of $\sqrt{(65)^2 - (16)^2}$
    a) 63
    b) 62
    c) 60
    d) 65

16. The length of the rectangle is twice its breadth. If its breadth be 'b', then its perimeter is
    a) 3b
    b) 6b
    c) $2b^2$
    d) $3b^2$

17. To a certain number 7 is added. The sum is multiplied by 5, the product is divided by 9 and 3 is subtracted from the quotient. If the remainder is 12, what is the number?
    a) 24
    b) 20
    c) 40
    d) 48

18. The length and breadth of a rectangular field are in the ratio of 5 : 3. It's area is 1500 sq.mts. Find the cost of fencing the field at Re.1 per metre.
    a) Rs.400
    b) Rs. 160
    c) Rs. 55
    d) Rs. 80

19. Raman invests a sum of Rs. 900 at 8% Simple Interest and Gopi invests a sum of Rs. 1200 at 3½% Simple Interest. After how much time will they both have equal amounts in their accounts?
    a) 20 years
    b) 30 years
    c) 40 years
    d) 10 years

20. A train, 180 m long, is running at a speed of 90 km/hr. How long will it take to pass railway signal?
    a) 72 seconds
    b) 7.2 seconds
    c) 27 seconds
    d) 2 seconds

21. If $\frac{a}{b} = \frac{1}{3}$, then $\frac{5a + b}{5a - b}$ equal to
    a) 4
    b) $\frac{16}{14}$
    c) $\frac{14}{16}$
    d) $\frac{1}{4}$

22. If $0.5 \times A = 0.0003$, then the value of A will be
    a) 0.6
    b) 0.06
    c) 0.006
    d) 0.0006

23. A vendor bought lemon at the rate of 6 for a rupee. How many for a rupee must he sell to gain 20%?
    a) 5
    b) 4
    c) 3
    d) 6

24. The square root of 0.0081 will be
    a) 0.009
    b) 0.09
    c) 0.0009
    d) 0.9

25. The value of
    $$\sqrt{16 + \sqrt{80 + \sqrt{5000 - 4999}}} \quad \text{will be}$$
    a) 5
    b) 13
    c) $\sqrt{97}$
    d) 9

• TEST No. 9 •

General Knowledge

1. Where is the Indian Institute of Astrophysics located?
   a) Thiruvanathapuram
   b) Chennai
   c) Bangalore   d) New Delhi

2. Election commission is a/an
   a) constitutional body
   b) legal body
   c) executive committee
   d) informal body

3. On which of the following rivers is Almati Dam located?
   a) Mahanadi   b) Cauvery
   c) Penganga   d) Krishna

4. Ship-building industry is mainly located in
   a) Mumbai   b) Kandla
   c) Vishakhapatnam   d) Calicut

5. Taj Mahal is on the banks of the river
   a) Ganges   b) Jamuna
   c) Sind   d) Tapti

6. Indian Standard Time (I.S.T.) is the local time of
   a) Delhi   b) Chennai
   c) Allahabad   d) Kolkata

7. Tamilnadu Sampark Kranthi Express runs between .... and ....
   a) Delhi, Coimbatore b) Delhi, Chennai
   c) Delhi, Madurai
   d) Delhi, Tirunelveli

8. Tea is grown much in
   a) Assam   b) Kerala
   c) Gujarat   d) Karnataka

9. Professor Yashpal is a noted
   a) Artist   b) Actor
   c) Scientist   d) Politician

10. 'Nilgiri' mountains are in
    a) Karnataka   b) Rajasthan
    c) Maharashtra   d) Tamil Nadu

11. Windows '95 is a
    a) Computer Software
    b) Computer Hardware

    c) Fancy Furniture
    d) None of these

12. 'Roentgen' discovered
    a) X-rays
    b) Encephalograph
    c) Anti-Polio Vaccine d) None of these

13. The President of India can contest for
    a) Two terms
    b) Three terms
    c) Any number of terms
    d) None of these

14. The gas used in an electric bulb is
    a) Nitrogen   b) Hydrogen
    c) Oxygen   d) Inert gas

15. 'Ptyalin' is an enzyme found in the
    a) saliva   b) bile
    c) blood   d) None of these

16. The place where Tower of Victory is located is
    a) Chittore   b) Udaipur
    c) Kota   d) Alwar

17. Where from 'Satyameva Jayate' is taken?
    a) Mundaka Upanishad
    b) Mahabharata
    c) Thirukkural
    d) Artha Shastra

18. How many districts are there in Tamil Nadu?
    a) 32   b) 28
    c) 29   d) 31

19. The Supreme Commander of the Armed Forces is
    a) The President   b) Chief Army Staff
    c) Field Marshall   d) Prime Minister

20. The Governor is appointed by
    a) The President   b) Prime Minister
    c) Law Minister   d) Chief Minister

21. Which day is observed as Teachers' Day?
    a) September 8   b) September 5
    c) November 14   d) August 15

22. The Lok Sabha member must have completed the age of
    a) 21 years   b) 25 years
    c) 30 years   d) 35 years

23. Who is the author of the book 'Panchali Sabadham'?
    a) Sundaram Pillai   b) Sekkizhar
    c) Andal   d) Bharathiyar

24. The term of the President of India is
    a) 3 years   b) 5 years
    c) 4 years   d) 7 years

25. Who wrote the Tamil hymn 'Thevaaram'?
    a) Manickavasagar
    b) Thirunavukkarasar
    c) Bharathiyar
    d) Vallalar

Reasoning - General Intelligence

1. Which one of the four choices makes the best comparison? LIVED is to DEVIL as 6323 is to:
   a) 2336   b) 6232
   c) 3236   d) 3326

2. Which one of these four is least like the other three?
   a) Horse   b) Kangaroo
   c) Cow   d) Deer

3. Which number should come next? 144 121 100 81 64 ?
   a) 17   b) 19
   c) 36   d) 49

4. Even the most _____ rose has thorns.
   a) Ugly   b) Weathered
   c) Elusive   d) Noxious

5. HAND is to Glove as HEAD is to
   a) Hair   b) Hat
   c) Neck   d) Earring

6. is to ◯◯ as is to

   a) ◯◯   b)

   c)   d)

7. John likes 400 but not 300; he likes 100 but not 99; he likes 3600 but not 3700. Which does he like?
   a) 900   b) 1000
   c) 1100   d) 1200

8. A fallacious argument is:
   a) Misleading   b) Valid
   c) False   d) Necessary

9. If you rearrange the letters "VANDRUMTRI," you would have the name of a(n):
   a) Ocean   b) Country
   c) State   d) City

10. NASA received three messages in a strange language from a distant planet. The scientists studied the messages and found that "Necor Buldon Slock" means "Danger Rocket Explosion" and "Edwan Mynor Necor" means "Danger Spaceship Fire" and "Buldon Gimilzor Gondor" means "Bad Gas Explosion". What does "Slock" mean?
    a) Danger   b) Explosion
    c) Nothing   d) Rocket

11. If some Wicks are Slicks, and some Slicks are Snicks, then some Wicks are definitely Snicks. The statement is:
    a) True   b) False
    c) Neither   d) None of these

12. Ann is taller than Jill, and Kelly is shorter than Ann. Which of the following statements would be most accurate?
    a) Kelly is taller than Jill
    b) Kelly is shorter than Jill
    c) Kelly is as tall as Jill
    d) It's impossible to tell

13. A boy is 4 years old and his sister is three times as old as he is. When the boy is 12 years old, how old will his sister be?
    a) 16   b) 20
    c) 24   d) 28

14. Assume that these two statements are true: All brown-haired men have bad tempers. Larry is a brown-haired man. The statement Larry has a bad temper is:
    a) True   b) False
    c) Unable to determine
    d) None of these

15. Two girls caught 25 frogs. Lisa caught four times as many as Jen did. How many frogs did Jen catch?
    a) 4   b) 5
    c) 8   d) 10

16. Inept is the opposite of:
    a) Healthy   b) Deep
    c) Skillful   d) Sad

17. A car travelled 28 kilometres in 30 minutes. How many kilometres per hour was it travelling?
    a) 28   b) 36
    c) 56   d) 58

18. If all Zips are Zoodles, and all Zoodles are Zonkers, then all Zips are definitely Zonkers, the above sentence is logically:
    a) True   b) False
    c) Neither   d) None of these

19. Sue is both the 50th best and the 50th worst student at her school. How many students attend her school?
    a) 50   b) 75
    c) 99   d) 100

20. In a race from point X to point Y and back, Jack averages 30 miles per hour to point Y and 10 miles per hour back to point X.

Sandy averages 20 miles per hour in both directions. Between Jack and Sandy, who finished first?
    a) Jack   b) Sandy
    c) They tie   d) Neither

Directions (Qns. 21-25): In each question below five words or names are given. You have to find out which word or name will be the MIDDLE after the words or names are arranged in the alphabetical order.

21. a) Language   b) Linguistic
    c) Literature   d) Literary
    e) Land

22. a) Condition   b) Continent
    c) Control   d) Counting
    e) Cowboy

23. a) Mouth   b) Month
    c) Money   d) Marry
    e) Manual

24. a) Nation   b) National
    c) Nature   d) Natural
    e) Net

25. a) Long   b) Length
    c) Breadth   d) Bridge
    e) Lucky

General English

Directions (Qns. 1-2): Fill in the blanks with suitable prepositions in the following sentences.

1. The police wrongly charged him .... murder
   a) for   b) of
   c) about   d) with

2. I was delighted .... his unexpected arrival
   a) in   b) for
   c) of   d) at

Directions (Qns. 3-4): Vocabulary (Mark the correct meaning):

3. warrant
   a) argue   b) to justify
   c) arrest   d) long for

4. abbreviate
   a) amplify   b) shorton
   c) widen   d) elongate

Directions (Qns. 5-10): In the words given below if the spelling is right, put 'R', if wrong put 'W'.

5. supprise   6. insistent
7. preseverence   8. privilege
9. satellite   10. predictible

Directions (Qns. 11-14): Choose the word which is OPPOSITE in meaning to the word given in capital.

11. RIDDLE
    a) Mystery   b) Conundrum
    c) Lowly   d) Clue

12. DISCIPLINE
    a) Order   b) Systematic
    c) Indiscipline   d) Standing

13. KNOWN
    a) Gone   b) Sown
    c) John   d) Unknown

Directions (Qns. 14-15): Choose one word for the following expressions:

14. The changed gender of cock
    a) Bird
    b) Hen
    c) Peacock
    d) Pigeon

15. The plural number of fish is
    a) Fishing
    b) Fish
    c) Black-fish
    d) Fisheries

Directions (Qns. 16-17): Fill in the blanks using one of the words given below each sentence.

16. You can .... into the well and take the bucket out.
    a) shallow
    b) surface
    c) dive
    d) bottom

17. When you breathe in, your .... fill with air.
    a) breathe
    b) lungs
    c) occupy
    d) immediately

Directions (Qns. 18-20): Choose the word which is nearly the same in meaning as the word given in capitals.

18. ANNEX
    a) Add
    b) Low
    c) Copy
    d) Initial

19. CONGREGATION
    a) Association
    b) Progress
    c) Cry
    d) Weeping

20. MANSION
    a) Polish
    b) Forward
    c) Large residence
    d) Office

21. One of the following words has two meanings. It is
    a) Horse
    b) Bear
    c) Cat
    d) Monkey

Directions (Qns. 22-25): Form sentences using the following words.

22. opposite
23. admission
24. junction
25. ancient

Arithmetic - Numerical Ability

1. $5\dfrac{3}{5} \times 2\dfrac{1}{7} + 5\dfrac{1}{2} = ?$
    a) $17\dfrac{1}{2}$
    b) $9\dfrac{1}{2}$
    c) $20\dfrac{1}{2}$
    d) $17\dfrac{3}{4}$

2. $6\dfrac{1}{4} \div 1\dfrac{2}{3} - 1\dfrac{1}{3} = ?$
    a) $2\dfrac{1}{12}$
    b) $1\dfrac{1}{12}$
    c) $2\dfrac{5}{12}$
    d) $4\dfrac{5}{12}$

3. $8514 + 3028 + 1213 = ?$
    a) 12855
    b) 12755
    c) 12935
    d) 12665

4. $8888 + 888 - 88 = ?$
    a) 8088
    b) 9608
    c) 9678
    d) None of these

5. $5.6 \times 4.5 + 3.4 = ?$
    a) 123.24
    b) 73.6
    c) 57.54
    d) None of these

6. $560.25 - ? = 739.25 - 241.67$
    a) 62.67
    b) 72.07
    c) 421.27
    d) 52.07

7. $8\dfrac{2}{3} + 11\dfrac{1}{3} - ? = 12\dfrac{2}{5}$
    a) $7\dfrac{2}{5}$
    b) $8\dfrac{3}{5}$
    c) $6\dfrac{3}{5}$
    d) $7\dfrac{3}{5}$

8. 40% of 2400 + ?% of 600 = 50% of 3840
    a) 50
    b) 40
    c) 80
    d) None of these

9. $175 \times ? = 140\%$ of 1200
    a) 8.4
    b) 7.5
    c) 13.44
    d) 9.6

10. $18 \times 144 \div 12 \times ? = 1296$
    a) 4
    b) 6
    c) 8
    d) 2

11. Add:

$$
\begin{array}{r}
2 \; 6 \; 4 \; 7 \; 6 \\
7 \; 8 \; 2 \; 3 \; 4 \\
9 \; 7 \; 4 \; 6 \; 2 \\
3 \; 8 \; 6 \; 4 \; 3 \\
\hline
\end{array}
$$

a) 240185   b) 234715

c) 240815   d) 294805

12. $\sqrt{441} =$

a) 21   b) ± 21

c) 29   d) 20.9

13. $\left[\dfrac{1}{3} + \dfrac{1}{2}\right] \times \dfrac{3}{4}\left[\dfrac{2}{3}\right]$

a) 5/12   b) 1/12

c) 7/12   d) 3/10

14. $\dfrac{6}{7} \div \dfrac{8}{9}\left[\dfrac{1}{2} + \dfrac{1}{2} + \dfrac{1}{3}\right]$

a) 1/12   b) 12/33

c) 81/112   d) None of these

15. The simple interest on a certain sum is Rs. 1200 in 3 years and the compound interest in two years is Rs. 825/-. The rate of interest is

a) 5%   b) 6¼%

c) 7%   d) 4 & ⅓%

16. A man buys 10 articles for Rs. 8 and sells the articles at the rate of 1.25 per article. His gain per cent is

a) 50%   b) 56¼%

c) 20%   d) 19½%

17. $8\dfrac{16}{25}$ is 48% of ?

a) 38   b) 20

c) 18.5   d) None of these

18. If Rs. 91/- is divided among A, B, C in the ratio 1½ : 3⅓ : 2¾, B will get

a) Rs. 36

b) Rs. 40

c) Rs.45

d) Rs. 48

19. $\dfrac{\sqrt{.0000136}}{\sqrt{.003}} =$

a) 0.148522

b) 6.7330032

c) 0.06733

d) 4.21742

20. $6^{3^2} = ?$

a) 108

b) 324

c) 1296

d) 46656

21. Simple interest on Rs. 600 at 18% per annum for 9 months is

a) Rs. 108   b) Rs. 81

c) Rs. 91   d) Rs. 180

22. If A : B = 5 : 4, B : C = 8 : 35, then A : C will be

a) 1 : 7   b) 2 : 7

c) 3 : 7   d) 7 : 2

23. The square root of 0.0081 will be

a) 0.009

b) 0.09

c) 0.0009

d) 0.9

24. $8008 - 8000 \div 10.00 = ?$

a) 0.8

b) 80

c) 7208

d) 8000

25. The average of 9 numbers is 7 and the average of 7 other numbers is 9. What is the average of all numbers considered together?

a) 8

b) $7\dfrac{14}{16}$

c) $8\dfrac{15}{16}$

d) $8\dfrac{1}{2}$

•TEST No. 10•

General Knowledge

1. Short sight is called
   a) Hypermetropia   b) Hypometropia
   c) Myopia
   d) Power of accommodation

2. Unit of wavelength is
   a) kg   b) Angstrom
   c) Ms^{-1} d) second

3. The unit of work is
   a) watt   b) metre
   c) second   d) joule

4. _____ gas is used to purify drinking water.
   a) chlorine   b) bromine
   c) fluorine   d) astatine

5. DDT is used as
   a) insecticide   b) fungicide
   c) weedicide   d) herbicide

6. Human heart is _____ chambered.
   a) 2   b) 3
   c) 4   d) 5

7. Prime Minister is appointed by
   a) his party men
   b) the speaker of Lok Sabha
   c) the majority members of Lok Sabha
   d) the President of India

8. Our Constitution came into force on
   a) 26th Nov. 1949   b) 15th Aug. 1945
   c) 26th Jan. 1950   d) 31st Jan. 1952

9. The first citizen and the executive head of India is the
   a) Prime Minister
   b) President
   c) Vice-president
   d) Election Commissioner

10. National flag of India was presented on behalf of
    a) Indian National Congress
    b) The people of India
    c) The women of India
    d) None of these

11. Which is the Biggest ocean in the world?
    a) Pacific   b) Atlantic
    c) Arctic   d) Indian

12. Aryabhatta was launched from
    a) Russia   b) India
    c) China   d) Canada

13. According to the census of 2001, what is India's population?
    a) 406.3 million
    b) 1028 million
    c) 987.8 million
    d) 596.2 million

14. The name of the super computer that launched by India is
    a) Dhara   b) Param Padama
    c) Lakshya   d) Indus-1

15. Who is India's Chief of Air-staff?
    a) Fauli H. Major
    b) Arun Prakash
    c) S.P. Tyagi
    d) Padmanabhan

16. Which day was celebrated on 11th July 2004?
    a) World Population Day
    b) International Day of Families
    c) No-Tobacco Day
    d) World Food day

17. Which of the following is the oldest library in India?
    a) Connemara Library, Chennai
    b) Central Reference Library, Kolkata
    c) Asiatic Society Library, Kolkata
    d) Delhi Public Library, Delhi

18. What is the name of the light passenger aircraft designed by India, that made its maiden flight on 29th May 2004?
    a) Lakshya   b) Saras
    c) Vayudoot   d) Virat

19. Cash crop does not include
    a) Sugarcane   b) Wheat
    c) Jute   d) Cotton

20. Who was the first India-born American woman to travel in space?
    a) Anjali Bhagwat   b) Kalpana Chawla
    c) Malleswari   d) Sania Mirza

21. How many General Elections were held so far in India?
    a) 15 .   b) 14
    c) 13   d) 12

22. Which is the correct duration of Eleventh Five Year Plan?
    a) 1955-60   b) 2007-12
    c) 2002-07   d) 1997-2002

23. Chandrayaan-1 was launched on
    a) 8.5.2008   b) 20.8.2008
    c) 22.10.2008   d) 18.7.2008

24. The density of population in India per sq.km as per 2001 Census was
    a) 156   b) 235
    c) 198   d) 325

25. Who is the speaker of the Lok Sabha?
    a) Somnath Chatterjee
    b) P.M. Sayeed
    c) Soli Sorabjee
    d) Bhairon Singh Shekawat

Reasoning - General Intelligence

Directions (Qns. 1-3): In each of the following questions select the similar pair as related to that given in the question.

1. Austria: Vienna :: ?
    a) Finland : Greece   b) Kenya : Nairobi
    c) Sofia : Bulgaria   d) Haiti : Guinea

2. Carpenter : Saw :: ?
    a) Author : Paper   b) Gardener : Chisel
    c) Tailor : Needle   d) Chisel : Sculptor

3. Son : Daughter :: ?
    a) Uncle : Mother   b) Earl : Pearl
    c) Sow : Pig   d) Bull : Mare

Directions (Qns. 4-6): In each of the following questions four items are given; out of which three are alike in a certain way and hence form a group. Find out, which one item is different?

4. a) Magazine   b) Book
    c) Library   d) Dictionary

5. a) Doctor   b) Dancer
    c) Singer   d) Painter

6. a) 3613   b) 5495
    c) 3245   d) 6396

7. Raj starts walking straight towards East. After walking 75 metres he turns to the left and walks 25 metres straight. Again he turns to left, walks a distance of 40 metres straight, again he turns to left, walks a distance of 25 metres. How far is he from the starting point?
    a) 25 metres   b) 140 metres
    c) 50 metres   d) None of these

8. How many 5s are there in the following number series which are preceded by 6 and followed by 7?
    3 1 2 4 5 6 7 5 6 5 7 2 4 7 5 6 6 5 7 4 5 7 6 5 3
    a) One   b) Five
    c) Four   d) Two

9. A is to the southwest of B, C is to the east of A and south-east of B and D is to the north of C. In which direction of B is D located?
    a) West   b) East
    c) North   d) South

10. You can get the name of a capital city by rearranging the letter group NCHADRHGIA. Which of the following are the first and the last letters respectively of the word?
    a) D and N   b) C and D
    c) G and H   d) C and H

11. The average age of 33 boys in a class and the class teacher is 14 years. If the age of class teacher is 47 years, what would be the average age of boys only?
    a) 10 years   b) 11 years
    c) 13 years   d) 12 years

Directions (Qns. 12 & 13): In each of the following questions what should come in the place of question-mark (?) in the given number series?

12. 511, 342, 463, 382, 431, 406, ?
    a) 401   b) 415
    c) 418   d) 444

13. 7, 11, 8, 12, 9, 13, ?
    a) 10
    b) 11
    c) 14
    d) 15

14. The following is folded in the shape of a cube. What will be its shape after folding? Find out from the given alternatives.

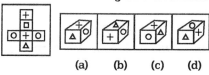

    (a)   (b)   (c)   (d)

Directions (Qns. 15-16): From the given responses find out the odd figure.

15.

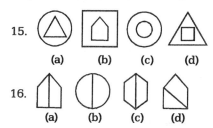

    (a)   (b)   (c)   (d)

16.

    (a)   (b)   (c)   (d)

17. Which number is opposite to the number 3?

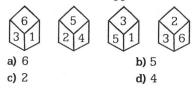

    a) 6
    b) 5
    c) 2
    d) 4

18. A is the brother of B, C is the sister of A, D is the brother of L, L is the daughter of B, then who is the uncle of D?
    a) B
    b) C
    c) A
    d) Cannot be determined

19. Ram can do a work in 6 days and Radhika can do the same work in 12 days. In how many days they will complete the work working together?

20. Sindhu borrowed Rs. 100 from Gokul. Komal borrowed Rs. 330 from Sindhu and Rs. 50 from Gokul. Rs. 400 was stolen from Gokul and he was left with no money. How much money did Gokul have initially?
    a) Rs. 550
    b) Rs. 600
    c) Rs. 500
    d) Rs. 350

21. Ram does not wear white dress and Arun does not wear blue dress. Ram and Shyam wear different coloured dresses. Only Sunder wears red dress. If everyone wears different coloured dresses, then what is the colour of Shyam's dress?
    a) White
    b) Red
    c) Blue
    d) None of these

22. Pointing at Govind, Gopal said, "His father is my father's son". Then what is the relation of Gopal to Govind?
    a) Father
    b) Son
    c) Grandfather
    d) Grandson

23. In a row of trees, a tree is at the 5th place from both the ends. How many trees are there in the row?
    a) 10
    b) 11
    c) 9
    d) 8

24. If ALTERED is written as ZOGVIVW, how would you write the word RELATED in the same code?
    a) IVOZGWV
    b) IVOZGVW
    c) VIOGZVW
    d) VOIZGVW

25. Which number comes next in the series 5, 16, 49, 104, ?
    a) 181
    b) 161
    c) 115
    d) 141

General English

Directions (Qns. 1-3): Mark the part in which the Grammatical mistake is:

. The firemen could not / succeed in rescue the /
         (a)   (b)
   child although they / could put out the fire.
         (c)   (d)

2. The student could not answer the teacher/
                            (a)
   when he was asked to explain /
                   (b)
   why he was so late that day / No error.
           (c)   (d)

3. If I would be a millionaire / I would not
       (a)   (b)
   be wasting my time / waiting for a bus /
                                      (c)
   No error.
       (d)

Directions (Qns. 4-5): Collective nouns: Pick out the correct nouns from the words given:

4. The navy show was highlighted by the exhibition of a line of _____ of boats.
   a) line   b) fight
   c) flotilla   d) troop

5. The hunter had a ____ of arrows in his quiver.
   a) bunch   b) set
   c) sheaf   d) faggot

Directions (Qns. 6-8): Supply suitable Prepositions from the given ones (where needed) in the blank spaces in the following sentences.

6. I wonder if I shall get _____ the history examination.
   a) about   b) out
   c) through   d) upon

7. You should adapt yourself _____ the conditions of this place.
   a) to   b) win
   c) on   d) for

8. Did you put those packages in the drawer or _____ the shelf?
   a) in   b) of
   c) on   d) about

Directions (Qns. 9-11): Choose the correct Word or Phrase:

9. He was _____ my hand so tightly that I could not pull it away.
   a) catching   b) holding
   c) seizing   d) none of these

10. Brevity is the soul of _____
    a) imagination   b) eloquence
    c) wit   d) mankind

11. After a _____ of several months the runaway boy turned up.
    a) passage   b) gap
    c) lapse   d) break

Directions (Qns. 12-14): Vocabulary (Mark the correct meaning):

12. Indifferent
    a) antipathetic   b) pathetic
    c) apathetic   d) none of these

13. prevalent
    a) dangerous   b) catching
    c) widespread   d) fatal

14. atheist
    a) believer in religion
    b) disbeliever in God
    c) bachelor
    d) believer in science

Directions (Qns. 15-17): Mark the correct Antonym of:

15. abiding
    a) permanent   b) existing
    c) passing   d) running

16. ample
    a) sufficient   b) wide
    c) ugly   d) insufficient

17. barren
    a) childless   b) beautiful
    c) plantless   d) fertile

Directions (Qns. 18-20): Fill in the gaps in the following sentences with the missing words choosing from the alternatives. The first letter/ letters and the meaning of each word are given to help you choose the required words.

18. The p_____ is so clear that it needs no explanation. (statement)
    a) problem   b) proposition
    c) position   d) property

19. Growing children should be given wh_____ food. (promoting good health)
    a) wheat   b) whole
    c) wholesome   d) whitebread

20. The victorious team was welcomed with ac_____ (shouts of applause)
    a) accord   b) acclaim
    c) acceptance   d) acknowledgement

Directions (Qns. 21-22): Substitute one word for the following:

21. Words having the opposite meaning _____

22. Incapable of being read _____

Directions (Qns. 23-25): Give the other tense forms:

	Present	Past	Past Participle
23.	—	Blew	—
24.	Hide	—	—
25.	—	—	Worn

Arithmetic - Numerical Ability

1. Which of the following numbers is the largest?
   a) $(2+2+2)^2$
   b) $\{(2+2)^2\}^2$
   c) $(2 \times 2 \times 2)^2$
   d) $2+2^2+(2)^2$

2. It cost Rs. 1,000 to make the first 1,000 copies of a book and X rupees to make each subsequent copy. If it costs a total of Rs. 7,230 to make the first 8,000 copies of a book, what is X?
   a) 0.89
   b) 0.90375
   c) 1
   d) 89

3. $1\dfrac{1}{4}(?) = \dfrac{1}{2}$
   a) $\dfrac{2}{5}$
   b) $\dfrac{5}{8}$
   c) $1\dfrac{3}{5}$
   d) $2\dfrac{1}{2}$

4. The average salary per head of all workers of an institution is Rs. 60. Average salary per head of 12 officers is Rs. 400. The average salary per head of the rest is Rs. 56. Find the total number of workers in the institution.
   a) 42
   b) 1,000
   c) 1,040
   d) 1,032

5. In a kilometre race, A can beat B by 20 metres while in a 500 metres race B can beat C by 15 metres. By what distance will A beat C in a 100 metres race?
   a) 4.94 metres
   b) 5.14 metres
   c) 6.24 metres
   d) 7.46 metres

6. The total weight of three children is 152 pounds and 4 ounces. The average weight is 50 pounds and how many ounces? (16 ounces = 1 pound)
   a) $\dfrac{1}{3}$ ounces
   b) $\dfrac{1}{2}$ ounces
   c) $1\dfrac{1}{3}$ ounces
   d) 12 ounces

7. If 4 men or 7 boys can do a work in 29 days, then what time will 12 men and 8 boys take to do the same work?
   a) 7
   b) 9
   c) 11
   d) 13

8. If $a + \dfrac{1}{a} = 5$ then $a^2 + \dfrac{1}{a^2} = ?$
   a) 23
   b) 25
   c) 27
   d) 0

9. If $(a+b+c) = 0$ then $a^3+b^3+c^3 = ?$
   a) abc
   b) 3abc
   c) 37abc
   d) a+b+c

10. 40 grams can be written in kilograms as
    a) 0.004
    b) 0.04
    c) 0.41
    d) 40

11. When 75% of a number is added to 75, then the result is the number again. The number is given by
    a) 100
    b) 200
    c) 250
    d) 300

12. $A : B = 4 : 5$; $B : C = 3 : 8$; $A : C = ?$
    a) 4 : 5
    b) 12 : 40
    c) 8 : 5
    d) 5 : 8

13. Divide Rs. 8,100 to A, B, C such that 1/2 of A's share, 1/3 of B's share and 1/4 of C's share are equal. Then A's share is
    a) Rs. 1,000
    b) Rs. 1,500
    c) Rs. 1,800
    d) Rs. 240

14. If some articles are bought at prices ranging from Rs. 200 to Rs. 350 and are sold at prices ranging from Rs. 300 to Rs. 425, what is the maximum possible profit that might be made in selling 16 such articles?
    a) Rs. 1,600
    b) Rs. 1,200
    c) Rs. 800
    d) Rs. 400

15. A farmer took a loan at 12% p.a. at S.I. After 4 years he settled the loan by paying Rs. 2,442. What was the principal amount?
    a) Rs. 1,542
    b) Rs. 1,600
    c) Rs. 1,650
    d) Rs. 1,550

16. A boat can be rowed 9 km upstream or 18 km downstream in a period of 3 hours. What is the speed of the boat in still water in km/hr?
    a) 1.5
    b) 3
    c) 4.5
    d) 6

17. Find the missing number: 1, 4, 7, 10.......
    a) 13
    b) 12
    c) 14
    d) None of these

18. The H.C.F of two numbers is 11 and their L.C.M. is 7700. If one of the number is 275, the other is
    a) 279
    b) 283
    c) 308
    d) 318

19. Simplify: $\dfrac{0.46 - 0.046}{0.046 \div 4.6}$
    a) 0.414
    b) 4.14
    c) 41.4
    d) None of these

20. $\dfrac{(7.59)^2 - (5.23)^2}{3 - 0.64} = ?$
    a) 12.28
    b) 12.82
    c) 18.12
    d) 18.21

21. $\sqrt{\dfrac{0.361}{0.00169}}$ is equal to
    a) $\dfrac{19}{30}$
    b) $\dfrac{1.9}{3}$
    c) $\dfrac{19}{13}$
    d) $\dfrac{190}{13}$

22. If 10% of x = 20% of y, then x : y = ?
    a) 1 : 2
    b) 2 : 1
    c) 2: 3
    d) 3 : 2

23. The average of first 50 natural numbers is
    a) 12.25
    b) 21.25
    c) 25
    d) 25.50

24. 40 is what percent of 1200?
    a) 3
    b) $3\dfrac{1}{3}$
    c) $6\dfrac{2}{3}$
    d) 6

25. The ratio of two numbers is 3 : 7. If 12 is subtracted from each, then the ratio becomes 9 : 37. The second number is
    a) 42
    b) 49
    c) 56
    d) 63

• TEST No. 11 •

General Knowledge

1. Silent valley national park is in _____
   a) Karnataka
   b) Kashmir
   c) Uttaranchal
   d) Kerala

2. Botanical name of India's National fruit is
   a) Mussaccous Sapientum
   b) Cirtus Sinensis
   c) Magnifera Indica
   d) Carica Papaya

3. Titan is the satellite of
   a) Saturn
   b) Earth
   c) Mars
   d) Pluto

4. What is the scientific name of "Kesari Dal"?
   a) Lathyrus Sativus
   b) Castanea Sativa
   c) Sarica Indica
   d) Melia Azerdarach

5. Proteins are
   a) Poly acids
   b) Poly Saccharides
   c) Peptides
   d) Poly Peptides

6. The acid present in Apple is
   a) Oxalic acid
   b) Lactic acid
   c) Malic acid
   d) Tartaric acid

7. Which one of the following is a modified stem?
   a) Carrot
   b) Beetroot
   c) Potato
   d) Turnip

8. Gravimeter is the instrument used to find the
   a) speed of ships
   b) oil deposits under water
   c) density of liquid
   d) gravity of liquids

9. Which one of the following is not an alloy?
   a) Copper
   b) Bronze
   c) Pewter
   d) Brass

10. Which part of our body is affected by the consumption of alcohol?
    a) Brain
    b) Spinal cord
    c) Legs
    d) Heart

11. "Our Father of Nation", Mahatma Gandhiji's samadhi is known as
    a) Abhay ghat
    b) Kisan ghat
    c) Raj ghat
    d) Vijay ghat

12. Who first referred Mahatma Gandhiji as "Father of the Nation"?
    a) Jawaharlal Nehru   b) Subash Chandra Bose
    c) Vallabhai Patel   d) Rajaji

13. Who among the following is called born builder?
    a) Jahangir   b) Akbar
    c) Babur   d) Shah Jahan

14. Raja Kesari, Arul Mozhi, and Mummudi Chozhan are the titles given to
    a) Raja Raja   b) Rajendra Chola
    c) Kulothunga Chola   d) Virarajendra

15. The silver coins issued by the Gupta's were called_____
    a) Pana   b) Karsha Pana
    c) Rupaka   d) Damara

16. Where is the headquarters of the three wings of the armed forces?
    a) Bangalore   b) Ranchi
    c) Mumbai   d) Delhi

17. _____ is called "The Island of Cloves".
    a) Newzealand   b) Guinea
    c) Zanzibar   d) Mauritius

18. Pankaj Advani is associated with
    a) Hockey   b) Chess
    c) Golf   d) Snooker

19. Shoaib Akhtar is popularly known as
    a) Pak Express   b) Pak Missile
    c) Thunder storm   d) Rawalpindi Express

20. Who is the first Indian girl to have won a Grand slam Title?
    a) Anjali Bhagwat   b) Kunja Rani
    c) Sania Mirza   d) Menaka Deol

21. Kabini dam was in News recently is located in
    a) Kerala   b) Tamil Nadu
    c) Karnataka   d) Andhra

22. The Minister (Cabinet Minister) for Communication and Information Technology is
    a) Mr. Anbumani Ramdoss
    b) Mr. T.R.Balu
    c) Mr. Dayanidhi Maran
    d) Mr. A. Raja

23. Name the first indigeneously assembled T-90 S Main Battle Tank.
    a) Arjun   b) Bhima
    c) Bhishma   d) Tarang

24. Name the animal indicated by WHO Expert as the prime suspect in spread of SARS.
    a) Monkey   b) Wolf
    c) Civet cat   d) Chicken

25. Who is the author of the book *A Tale of Two cities*?
    a) D.H. Lawrence
    b) Charles Dickens
    c) R.L. Stevenson
    d) William Shakespeare

Reasoning - General Intelligence

1. Find out the one which is different from others.
   a) Tomato   b) Potato
   c) Carrot   d) Onion

2. Which one number will complete the following number series?
   5   7   11   17   25   ?
   a) 29   b) 32
   c) 35   d) 37

3. Which word cannot be formed from the letters of the following word?
   ETHNOGRAPHIC
   a) EARTH   b) HEART
   c) TIGER   d) GARMENT

4. If BAROMETERS is written in a code as "MORABSRETE", DENDROLOGY may be written in the same code as
   a) EDDNOROLYG
   b) DNEDOLYGO
   c) RDNEDYGOLO
   d) RDNEDYGOOL

5. Which would be the proper order of the following?
   1) Country   2) Furniture
   3) Forest   4) Wood
   5) Trees
   a) 24315   b) 14325
   c) 52314   d) 13542

6. If "INDIA" is coded as FKAFX then "MADRAS" will be coded as
   a) MXARXS
   b) NXSAXT
   c) JXAOXP
   d) XOAMPX

7. How many 4's are there in the following series which are preceded by 9 but are not preceded by 6?

   4 9 3 6 7 9 4 6 3 2 6 4 1 9 4 6 3
   5 8 9 4 6

   a) One
   b) Two
   c) Three
   d) Four

8. Arrange the following words according to the Dictionary.
   1) Exodus   2) Exotic
   3) Exogamy   4) Exonerate
   a) 1432
   b) 1342
   c) 1234
   d) 4213

Directions (Qns. 9-12): Groups of four words are given. In each group, one word is misspelt. Find the misspelt word.

9. a) Shoddy   b) Seeming
   c) Sculpter   d) Shellac

10. a) Pronominel   b) Pursue
    c) Pyorrhoea   d) Personage

11. a) Misappropriation b) Malignant
    c) Mantel   d) Marginate

12. a) Unequipped   b) Unenduring
    c) Unmindfull   d) Utilize

13. A Family has a man, his wife, their 4 sons and their wives. The Family of every son also have 3 sons and one daughter each. Find out the total number of male members.
    a) 1
    b) 12
    c) 4
    d) 17

14. How many triangles are there in the figure?

    a) 16
    b) 12
    c) 10
    d) 8

15. Which number is opposite of 2?

    a) 3
    b) 4
    c) 5
    d) 6

16. I walked 3 km towards south and turned to my left and walked 5 km. Again, I turned to my right and walked 7 km. Finally in which direction I was walking?
    a) South
    b) South-East
    c) East
    d) West

17. In certain code Yellow is called White, White is called Blue, Blue is called Red, Red is called Pink. What is the colour of Blood?
    a) Red
    b) Blue
    c) Pink
    d) White

Directions (Qns. 18-20): Insert the missing number at the sign of interrogation.

18.
1	2	3
11	7	5
120	45	?

    a) 15
    b) 16
    c) 17
    d) 19

19.
3	4	5
3	7	12
3	?	22

    a) 8
    b) 9
    c) 10
    d) 11

20. 2, 5, 10, 17, 26 ?
    a) 53
    b) 43
    c) 36
    d) 37

Directions (Qns. 21-22): Choose the related word out of the options given below.

21. Mound : Height :: Trench?
    a) Sea
    b) Deep
    c) Depth
    d) Stripe

22. Papers : File :: Stick :?
    a) Faggot
    b) Cannonnade
    c) Rope
    d) Bunch

23. **Chant : Sing :: Chatter :?**
    a) Play
    b) Shout
    c) Noise
    d) Talk

24. **Psychology : Mind :: Ornithology?**
    a) Coin
    b) Mammal
    c) Eggs
    d) Birds

25. **ITEM : MITE :: ACHE?**
    a) HEAC
    b) HECA
    c) EACH
    d) CEHA

General English

Directions (Qns. 1-3): Choose one alternative which gives the exact meaning of the given word.

1. **Adjust**
   a) Suitable
   b) Balance
   c) Harmonise
   d) Admit

2. **Massacre**
   a) Slaughter
   b) Stab
   c) Killing
   d) Murder

3. **Ghastly**
   a) Grimy
   b) Fraud
   c) Viscid
   d) Horrible

Directions (Qns. 4-6): Choose one alternative which gives the exact OPPOSITE of the given word.

4. **Blackguard**
   a) Gentleman
   b) Assistant
   c) Whiteguard
   d) Noble

5. **Gather**
   a) Separate
   b) Suspend
   c) Scatter
   d) Disperse

6. **Innocent**
   a) Sinful
   b) Quiet
   c) Wickedness
   d) Guilty

Directions (Qns. 7-10): Group of four words are given. In each group one word is misspelt. Find the word.

7. a) BELIEVE
   b) DECIEVE
   c) HAIVE
   d) LITERARY

8. a) ALLERGY
   b) ADMIROR
   c) PROPRIETOR
   d) SYLLABLE

9. a) DEFINATION
   b) DETERMINATION
   c) CULMINATION
   d) TERMINATION

10. a) ANXIETY
    b) HACK
    c) ANKEL
    d) ACQUIRED

Directions (Qns. 11-14): Some sentences are given; in which you have to fill in the blanks with suitable Prepositions.

11. **There is no difference _____ the Jews and the Greeks.**
    a) among
    b) in
    c) between
    d) with

12. **Hydrogen has some advantage _____ hot air.**
    a) upon
    b) in
    c) over
    d) with

13. **The machine was put in place _____ the rail.**
    a) upon
    b) over
    c) along
    d) within

14. **He lost control _____ his bike.**
    a) on
    b) in
    c) over
    d) with

Directions (Qns. 15 and 16): Identify the types of sentences.

15. **Please keep off the grass**
    a) Statement
    b) Imperative
    c) Exclamatory
    d) Interrogative

16. **I came late to school.**
    a) Statement
    b) Imperative
    c) Exclamatory
    d) Interrogative

Directions (Qns. 17-20): Identify the sentence patterns.

17. **The Judge found him innocent.**
    a) S-V-C
    b) S-V-IO-DO
    c) S-V-O-A
    d) S-V-O-C

18. **The Teacher scolded angrily.**
    a) S-V-C
    b) S-V-A
    c) S-V-O
    d) S-A-C

19. **He drives the car very fastly.**
    a) S-O-A
    b) S-V-O-C
    c) S-V-A-C
    d) S-V-IO-DO

20. He answered the question well
    a) S-V-O-C
    b) S-O-A
    c) S-O-C
    d) S-V-O-A

Directions (Qns. 21-25): Make your own sentences using the given words.

21. Urged   22. Knave

23. Impart   24. Sob

25. Wrest

Arithmetic - Numerical Ability

1. Simplify : $1\dfrac{7}{9} \times \dfrac{9}{20} + 2\dfrac{5}{8} \times 1\dfrac{1}{15}$

   a) $\dfrac{5}{18}$ b) $\dfrac{18}{5}$

   c) $\dfrac{2}{5}$ d) $\dfrac{5}{2}$

2. Divide: $3\dfrac{12}{17} \div 1\dfrac{11}{34}$

   a) 14   b) $\dfrac{8}{5}$

   c) $2\dfrac{4}{5}$ d) $4\dfrac{2}{5}$

3. Determine the value: $20 \div (2 + \overline{5 - 3})$
   a) 6   b) 5
   c) 4   d) 3

4. If a car is running at a speed of 60 km per hour, how much time will it take to reach a destination which is 72 km from the starting point.
   a) 1 hour 20 min   b) 45 min
   c) 1 hour 45 min   d) 1 hour 2 min

5. What distance will a person travel in 4 hours if he maintains a speed of 15 m/sec?
   a) 600 km   b) 160 km
   c) 216 km   d) 260 km

6. What percent is 22 of 40?
   a) 40   b) 44
   c) 45   d) 55

7. $\dfrac{6}{18} \div ? = 18$

   a) 54   b) $\dfrac{1}{54}$

   c) $\dfrac{1}{36}$ d) 36

8. Find the square root: $\sqrt{4562}$
   a) 66.52   b) 67.52
   c) 66.53   d) 67.54

9. If 25% of a certain number of apples are rotten and the number of rotten apples are 700, find the total number of apples.
   a) 3000   b) 2900
   c) 2800   d) 2705

10. $\left(999^2 - 998^2\right) \div 20 \times 100 + 40 = ?$
    a) 1025   b) 10025
    c) 100025   d) 1250

11. What is the least number between 50 and 100 which is fully divisible by 3, 6 and 15?
    a) 70   b) 60
    c) 55   d) 80

12. A candidate scoring 20% marks in an exam fails by 30 marks and another candidate who scores 32% marks gets 42 marks more than those required to pass. Find the total maximum marks.
    a) 500   b) 600
    c) 750   d) 800

13. The volume of a Right circular cone of height 12 cm and base radius 60 cm is
    a) 12 π b) 36 π
    c) 72 π d) 144 π

14. If the cost price of 12 pens is equal to selling price of 10 pens, then find the gain or loss percentage of the selling price.
    a) 10% gain   b) 20% loss
    c) 20% gain   d) 15% loss

15. A wheel makes 1000 revolutions in covering a distance of 83 km. The diameter of the wheel is
    a) 24 m   b) 14 m
    c) 40 m   d) 28 m

16. A merchant marks his goods at Rs.300 and allows a discount of 25%. If he still gains 12.5%, then the cost of article is
a) 200
b) 220
c) 240
d) 250

17. A, B, C hired a car for Rs. 520 and used it for 7, 8 and 11 hours respectively. Hire charges paid by "B" is
a) Rs.140
b) Rs.150
c) Rs.160
d) Rs.170

18. By how much is $\dfrac{4}{5}$ of 700 is greater than $\dfrac{5}{7}$ of 550?
a) 165
b) 167
c) 168
d) 166

19. The ratio between two numbers is 5:4. If 40% of the first number is 12, what is 50% of the second number?
a) 12
b) 24
c) 40
d) 28

20. $\dfrac{2}{5}$ of $\dfrac{1}{4}$ of $\dfrac{3}{7}$ of a number is 15. What is half of that number?
a) 45
b) 75
c) 145
d) 175

21. $1.542 \times 2408.69 + 1134.632 = ?$
a) 4488
b) 4846
c) 4848
d) 4858

22. 143% of $3015 + 1974 = 9500 - ?$
a) 3214.55
b) 3114.55
c) 3014.55
d) 3015.55

23. $9568 - 6548 - 1024 = ?$
a) 2086
b) 4044
c) 2293
d) 1996

24. $16\sqrt{49} + 1492 - 250.52 = ?$
a) 1353
b) 1463
c) 1368
d) 1343

25. $152\sqrt{?} + 795 = 8226 - 3400$
a) 746
b) 773.426
c) 703.31
d) 704.31

TEST No. 12

General Knowledge

1. World Literacy Day is observed on
a) September 8
b) December 13
c) December 23
d) December 30

2. With which sport is Sania Mirza related?
a) Shooting
b) Wrestling
c) Tennis
d) Weightlifting

3. India won the final match of Junior Asia Cup at Karachi after defeating
a) Srilanka
b) Australia
c) Pakistan
d) Bangladesh

4. Who is the first woman to be appointed as United Nations Civilian Police Adviser?
a) Kanchan Chowdhry
b) Meeran Borwankar
c) Kiran Bedi
d) Thilakavathy

5. The Education Satellite that was launched during the month of September 2004 is
a) Edubat
b) Edutiosat
c) EdIndia
d) Edusat

6. The Headquarters of ISRO is located in
a) Delhi
b) Bangalore
c) Kolkata
d) Mumbai

7. Name the country which has withheld its role in Srilanka Peace process.
a) UK
b) Denmark
c) Norway
d) USA

8. Dry ice is
a) Solid Carbon dioxide
b) Super-Cooled ice
c) Solid Ammonia
d) Solid water

9. The human body is immune to which of the following diseases?
   a) Small pox
   b) Jaundice
   c) Diabetes
   d) None

10. The number of ribs in human body is
    a) 18
    b) 22
    c) 24
    d) 26

11. Iodised salt contains
    a) Calcium iodide
    b) Potassium iodate
    c) Magnesium iodide
    d) Free iodine

12. The lightest particle of matter is
    a) Electron
    b) Proton
    c) Neutron
    d) Deuteron

13. Which of the following gases is present under pressure in soft drinks?
    a) Nitrogen
    b) Oxygen
    c) Carbon dioxide
    d) None of these

14. The Commander-in-chief of Siraj-ud-Daula was
    a) Mir Qasim
    b) Alivardi khan
    c) Shuja-ud-Daula
    d) Mir Jafar

15. The First Maratha War came to an end by
    a) The treaty of Srirangapatnam
    b) Mangalore treaty
    c) Treaty of Sagauli
    d) Treaty of Salbai

16. Who were the first kings to issue coins bearing their names?
    a) Kushans
    b) Mauryans
    c) Scythians
    d) Bactrians

17. The people of the Indus Valley Civilisation worshipped
    a) Pashupati
    b) Vishnu
    c) Brahma
    d) Indra and Varuna

18. Moplah revolt broke out in _____
    a) Bihar, 1924
    b) Bihar, 1921
    c) Kerala, 1924
    d) Kerala, 1921

19. Treaty of Mangalore was signed between
    a) the English East India Company & Haidar Ali
    b) the French & Haidar Ali
    c) the English East India Company & Tipu Sultan
    d) the French and Tipu Sultan

20. Which of the following is a Rice Research station in Thanjavur District?
    a) Thanjavur
    b) Aduthurai
    c) Thiruvarur
    d) Kumbakonam

21. Which one of the following pairs is not correctly matched?
    a) Chilka Lake - Orissa
    b) Pushkar Lake - Srinagar
    c) Vemanad Lake - Kerala
    d) Loktak Lake - Manipur

22. The Vice-president presides over the
    a) Lok Sabha
    b) Rajya Sabha
    c) Parliament
    d) Planning Commission

23. Whose signature is found on one rupee note?
    a) Governor of RBI
    b) Finance Minister
    c) Deputy Finance Minister
    d) Finance Secretary

24. Radcliff line is a boundary line between
    a) India & China
    b) India & Pakistan
    c) Pakistan & China
    d) Pakistan & Afghanistan

25. Who gave the slogan "Delhi Chalo"?
    a) Gandhiji
    b) Nehru
    c) Subash Chandra Bose
    d) S.V. Patel

Reasoning - General Intelligence

Directions (Qns. 1-2): Answer the following questions based on the letter number sequence given below.

    B 3 K G 5 P D 7 9 E R J
    I M T 6 Z H Q 8 W 2 A

1. Three of the following four are alike in a certain way with regard to their position in the above sequence. Which is the one that does not belong to the other four?
   a) 3GD
   b) IR7
   c) M6Q
   d) 6HW

2. What should come in the place of question mark (?)

| 3GP | D9R | JM6 | ? |

   a) ZHW
   b) ZQW
   c) 6HW
   d) M6Q

Directions (Qns. 3-7): Find the odd one.

3. a) 39   b) 63
   c) 83   d) 51

4. a) 216   b) 144
   c) 64   d) 81

5. a) Night   b) Sun
   c) Dawn   d) Asteroid

6. a) Calorie   b) Lactometer
   c) Farad   d) Mole

7. a) Room   b) Kitchen
   c) Floor   d) Bed Room

8. "Soldier" is related to army; in the same way as "pupil" is related to
   a) Teacher   b) Class
   c) Student   d) Education

9. If white is called Blue, Blue is called Red, Red is called Yellow, Yellow is called Green, Green is called Violet. What would be the colour of leaf?
   a) Red   b) Blue
   c) Violet   d) Green

10. In a certain code 'SUBSTITUTION' is written as 'ITSBUSNOITUT'. How is 'DISTRIBUTION' written in that code?
    a) IRTDISNOIUTB   b) IRTSIDNOITUB
    c) IRTSDNOIBUT   d) IRTSIDNOTIUB

11. If '–' means '×', '×' means '+', '+' means '÷' and '÷' means '–' then
    40 × 12 + 3 – 6 ÷ 60 = ?
    a) 44   b) 16
    c) 24   d) 4

Directions (Qns. 12-16): Find the correct alternative for the following questions from the four alternatives given below.

12. **Push : Pull :: Throw : ?**
    a) Collect   b) Catch
    c) Fall   d) None of these

13. **Ankle : Knee :: Wrist : ?**
    a) Finger   b) Hand
    c) Elbow   d) Foot

14. **DRIVE : EIDRV :: BEGUM : ?**
    a) BGMEU   b) MGBEU
    c) UEBGM   d) EUBGM

15. **Court : Judge :: School : ?**
    a) Teacher   b) Pupil
    c) Office Staff   d) Headmaster

16. **Disease : Medicine :: Famine : ?**
    a) Clouds   b) Rainfall
    c) Drought   d) River

Directions (Qns. 17-20): The second figure in the first unit of the problem figures bears a certain relationship to the first figure. Similarly one of the figures in the answer figures bears the relationship of the third figure. Find the figure which would fit the question mark.

17. **Problem Figures**

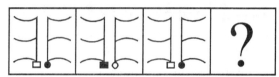

Answer Figures

(a)   (b)   (c)   (d)

18. **Problem Figures**

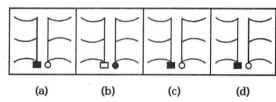

Answer Figures

(a)   (b)   (c)   (d)

19. **Problem Figures**

Answer Figures

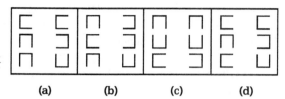

| (a) | (b) | (c) | (d) |

20. Problem Figures

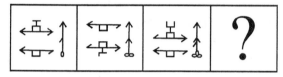

Answer Figures

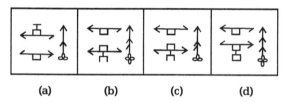

| (a) | (b) | (c) | (d) |

21. Insert the missing number
7, 15, 32, ?, 138, 281
a) 50   b) 64
c) 67   d) None

22. One morning after sunrise Gangadhar was standing facing a pole. The shadow of the pole fell exactly to his right. Which direction was he facing?
a) South   b) North
c) East   d) West

23. Ramu went 12 kms towards North and turned towards his left and walked 6 kms then turned right and walked 12 kms. and again turned right and walked 6 kms. How far he is from the starting point?
a) 36 km   b) 18 km
c) 30 km   d) 24 km

24. How many triangles are there in the given figure?

a) 2   b) 5
c) 7   d) 8

25. If A = 4, B = 5, PINK = 62, then RED = ?
a) 26   b) 39
c) 36   d) None of these

General English

Directions (Qns. 1-5): Select the suitable preposition for the blanks given.

1. We sailed _____ the river.
   a) down   b) at
   c) upon   d) over

2. The sky is _____ the earth.
   a) over   b) upon
   c) above   d) higher

3. _____ his children, there were relatives.
   a) Among   b) With
   c) Between   d) Besides

4. An exhibition _____ the new trends in computer education was held in Delhi.
   a) into   b) on
   c) for   d) in

5. The policemen swung into action and cordoned _____ the area.
   a) off   b) over
   c) near   d) in

Directions (Qns. 6-10): Choose the word of phrase nearest to similar in meaning to the underlined word.

6. The data is misleading.
   a) Illusory   b) Deceptive
   c) Misplaced   d) Talkative

7. In modern hospitals computers check the patients before they see the doctor.
   a) stop   b) see
   c) cover   d) screen

8. A genius tends to deviate from the routine way of thinking.
   a) Dispute   b) Distinguish
   c) Differ   d) Vary

9. Many educationists think that the classroom instruction should be made more <u>vigorous</u>.
   a) Serious
   b) Brisk
   c) Active
   d) Lively

10. Corruption <u>stalks</u> every sphere of national life.
   a) Poisons
   b) Pollutes
   c) Penetrates
   d) Pervades

Directions (Qns. 11-15): Rearrange the Jumbled Sentences:

11. <u>It is</u> that people read fewer books today (P) / than they did (Q) / even about a decade ago (R) / a matter of grave concern (S).
   a) SPQR
   b) SPRQ
   c) PQRS
   d) PSQR

12. <u>On seeing the tiger</u>, the lamb (P) / began to cry (Q) / which had lost its mother (R) / and tried to run away (S).
   a) PRSQ
   b) PRQS
   c) PQRS
   d) PQSR

13. <u>I told my friend</u> on the first of April (P) / that I was going to Germany (Q) whom I met at Nagpur (R) / at a conference in January (S).
   a) RSQP
   b) QPRS
   c) RPQS
   d) SQPR

14. <u>When the Sun rose</u> (P) / as his objective was to reach his destination (Q) / the traveller resumed his journey (R) / in time (S).
   a) SRQP
   b) PSRQ
   c) RQPS
   d) PRQS

15. <u>Kapil</u> left in an aeroplane (P) / after reading a sailing magazine (Q) / had decided (R) / to build his own boat nine years earlier (S).
   a) RSQP
   b) PSRQ
   c) RQPS
   d) PRQS

Directions (Qns. 16-18): Fill in the blanks with suitable question tag.

16. Don't come late _____ ?

17. Only a little improvement is seen _____ ?

18. I am a teacher, _____ ?

Directions (Qns. 19-20): Identify the sentence patterns.

19. Raju's father got him a new Watch. (S = Subject, V = Verb, IO = Indirect Object, DO = Direct Object)
   a) S+IO+DO
   b) S+V+O
   c) S+V+IO+DO
   d) S+V+O+C

20. Is he watching the TV?
   a) S+V+O
   b) V+IO+V+DO
   c) V+S+V+O
   d) V+S+V+C

Directions (Qns. 21-25): Rewrite the following sentences as directed.

21. Naresh said to me, "I like cherry." (Change into Indirect Speech)

22. The Police said to them, "Leave this place at once". (Change into Indirect Speech)

23. Do you love her? (Change into Passive Voice)

24. Because of studying well, she scored 1180 marks. (Change into Compound Sentence)

25. Balu is cleverer than many other boys. (Change into Positive Degree)

Arithmetic - Numerical Ability

1. If one-fifth of one-third of one-half of a number is 15, then find that number?
   a) $\dfrac{17}{2}$
   b) $\dfrac{240}{9}$
   c) 540
   d) 450

2. The sum of two numbers is twice their difference. If one of the number is 10 then the other number is _____
   a) 25
   b) 30
   c) 32
   d) 19

3. $10\dfrac{5}{6} \div 91 = ?$
   a) $\dfrac{42}{5}$
   b) $\dfrac{5}{42}$
   c) $\dfrac{15}{4}$
   d) $\dfrac{4}{15}$

4. Simplify: $\dfrac{1}{2+\dfrac{1}{3+\dfrac{1}{1+\dfrac{1}{4}}}}$

a) $\dfrac{12}{7}$

b) $\dfrac{43}{19}$

c) $\dfrac{7}{12}$

d) $\dfrac{19}{43}$

5. Find the value of $\dfrac{\sqrt{\left(\sqrt{5}+1\right)^2}}{5-1}$

a) 36

b) 6

c) 1.6

d) 6.1

6. If x = 12, y = 4, then find the value of $(x + y)^{x/y}$
   a) 48
   b) 64
   c) 496
   d) 4096

7. Find the three numbers in the ratio of 1:2:3 so that the sum of their square is equal to 504.
   a) 8 : 16 : 24
   b) 6 : 12 : 24
   c) 6 : 12 : 18
   d) 4 : 8 : 12

8. If 192 mangoes can be bought for Rs. 15, how many mangoes can be bought for Rs. 5?
   a) 65
   b) 75
   c) 62
   d) 64

9. A man invests 12½% of his salary in a business. If his annual salary is Rs. 50128, how much does he invest per annum?
   a) 4172
   b) 2426.50
   c) 6266
   d) 5292

10. The average age of 30 bags of a class is equal to 14 years. When the age of the class teacher is included, the average becomes 15 years. Find the age of the class teacher?
    a) 45
    b) 25
    c) 48
    d) 52

11. At what rate of compound interest per annum will a sum of Rs. 1200 become Rs. 1348.32 in 2 years?

a) 4%
b) 6%
c) 7.5%
d) None

12. The ratio of Vimal's age and Amala's age is in the ratio 3:5 and the sum of their age is 80 years. The ratio of their ages after 10 years will be ___
    a) 2 : 3
    b) 1 : 3
    c) 3 : 5
    d) 2 : 5

13. In an examination 1100 boys and 900 girls appeared. 50% of the boys and 40% of the girls passed the exams. The percentage of candidates failed is ___
    a) 54.5
    b) 45.4
    c) 75.4
    d) 44.5

14. Find the value of square root if $\dfrac{392}{\sqrt{?}} = 28$
    a) 24
    b) 48
    c) 144
    d) 196

15. The greatest possible length which can be used to measure exactly the lengths of 4 m, 95 cm, 9 m & 16 m 65 cm is
    a) 45 cm
    b) 25 cm
    c) 35 cm
    d) 15 cm

16. Imran sold a machine for Rs. 5060 at a gain of 10%. Find the cost price of the machine?
    a) 4820
    b) 4760
    c) 4609
    d) 4600

17. If oranges are bought at the rate of 30 for a rupee, how many must be sold for a rupee in order to gain 50%?
    a) 17
    b) 20
    c) 23
    d) 10

18. In how many years will Rs. 8500 amount to Rs. 15767.50 at 4½ per cent per annum?
    a) 19 years
    b) 17 years
    c) 15 years
    d) 12 years

19. A semi-circular shaped window has a diameter of 63 cm. Its perimeter equals.
    a) 162 cm
    b) 152 cm
    c) 172 cm
    d) 142 cm

20. Simplify: $\dfrac{31}{10} \times \dfrac{3}{10} + \dfrac{7}{5} \div 20 = ?$
    a) $\dfrac{1}{10}$
    b) 1
    c) 2
    d) 10

21. $\dfrac{\sqrt{625}}{11} \times \dfrac{14}{\sqrt{25}} \times \dfrac{11}{196} = ?$

    a) 6
    b) 8
    c) 5
    d) 7

22. $3 \div \left[(8-5) \div \left\{ (4-2) \div \left(2 + \dfrac{8}{13} \right) \right\} \right] = ?$

    a) $\dfrac{13}{17}$
    b) $\dfrac{17}{13}$
    c) $\dfrac{23}{17}$
    d) 24

23. Mean proportional between 7 and 28 is
    a) 14
    b) 12
    c) 16
    d) 17

24. Two pipes A and B can fill a tank in 36 hrs and 45 hrs respectively. If both the pipes are opened simultaneously how much time will be taken to fill the tank?

    a) $\dfrac{20}{7}$
    b) $\dfrac{180}{7}$
    c) $\dfrac{1}{20}$
    d) $\dfrac{4}{5}$

25. How many seconds will a train 100 metres long running at a speed of 36 km per hour take to pass a pole?
    a) 7 sec
    b) 9 sec
    c) 10 sec
    d) 12 sec

•TEST No. 13•

General Knowledge

1. Which State has the largest number of sugar mills?
   a) Tamil Nadu
   b) Uttar Pradesh
   c) Kerala
   d) Haryana

2. Which of the following is the first 'IT' district in the country?
   a) Mallapuram
   b) Chennai
   c) Palakkad
   d) Thrissur

3. UNESCO has declared the Airavatesvara temple of Darasuram as one of the 'World Heritage Monuments'. Where is the temple situated?
   a) Kerala
   b) Uttaranchal
   c) Tamilnadu
   d) Orissa

4. What was the name of the world's first cloned sheep that died recently?
   a) Bolly
   b) Dolly
   c) Colly
   d) Molly

5. Which of the following is NOT a form of precipitation?
   a) Fog
   b) Hail
   c) Snowfall
   d) Rainfall

6. What is the main constituent of Bio-diesel?
   a) Methanol
   b) Ethanol
   c) Methane
   d) Carbon

7. The Indian Olympic Association recently imposed life ban on three top weight lifters. Which of the following is NOT among them?
   a) S. Sunaina
   b) Karnam Malleswari
   c) Pratima Kumari
   d) Sanamacha Shanu

8. Which of the following films won maximum Oscar at the 80th Academy Awards (2008) in Los Angeles?
   a) Mystic River
   b) Lord of the Rings: The Return of the King
   c) Monster
   d) No Country for Old Men

9. Who of the following killed General Dyer, who was responsible for Jallianwala Bagh massacre?
   a) Prithvi Singh
   b) Udham Singh
   c) Sardar Singh
   d) Sohan Singh

10. Which Sikh Guru helped the rebel prince Khusro with money and blessings?
    a) Guru Hargovind
    b) Guru Govind Singh
    c) Guru Tegh Bahadur
    d) Guru Arjun Dev

11. Which is the official language of the state of Jammu and Kashmir?
    a) Kashmiri
    b) Hindi
    c) English
    d) Urdu

12. Which one of the following conditions causes rainfall?
    a) Cooling of the dry air
    b) Increase in humidity
    c) Cooling of the saturated air
    d) Decrease in humidity

13. If a person has 'Fear of Flying' it is called
    a) Aviophobia   b) Anthophobia
    c) Angrophobia   d) Acrophobia

14. Who appoints the Controller and Auditor-General of India?
    a) Prime Minister
    b) Chief Justice of Supreme Court
    c) President
    d) Speaker of Lok Sabha

15. Which of the following is the best fertilizer for plants?
    a) Urea   b) Super phosphate
    c) Sulphate   d) Compost

16. Which one of the following genetic diseases is sex-linked?
    a) Haemophilia   b) Hypertension
    c) Paralysis   d) Jaundice

17. Containers for carrying strong acids are made of
    a) Copper
    b) Lead
    c) Tin
    d) Brass

18. Anti-coagulant substance called 'Heparin' which helps in blood clotting is secreted by
    a) Platelets   b) Liver
    c) Intestine   d) Pituitary gland

19. Which one of the following pigments is used for making yellow paints?
    a) Basic Lead Carbonate
    b) Lead Oxide
    c) Chromic Oxide
    d) Lead Chromate

20. Australian Open Women's Singles (2009) title was won by
    a) Justine Henin-Hardenne
    b) Martina Hingis
    c) Serena Williams
    d) Maria Sharapova

21. What is 'Phycology'?
    a) Study of Fungus   b) Study of Virus
    c) Study of Plants   d) Study of Algae

22. Which of the following is the only country in the world with Hinduism as its state religion?
    a) India   b) Nepal
    c) Bhutan   d) Mauritius

23. Which of the following Indian naval ships became the first to complete a voyage around the world recently?
    a) INS Virat   b) INS Tarangini
    c) INS Maratha   d) None of these

24. What is the original name of Swami Ramakrishna Paramahamsa?
    a) Birendra Kumar
    b) Rakhal Banerjee
    c) Gadhadhar Chattopadhyaya
    d) Ramakrishnan

25. Botanical name of 'Tulasi' is
    a) Centella asiatica
    b) Triticum Vulgare
    c) Dalbergia latifolia   d) Ocimum Sanctum

Reasoning - General Intelligence

Directions (Qns. 1-5): Find the odd man out.

1. 45   52   61   72   86   100
    a) 52   b) 61
    c) 86   d) 100

2. 4   12   48   240   1110   10080
    a) 48   b) 240
    c) 1110   d) None of these

3. a) Post Master   b) Post Office
    c) Post Card   d) Post Box

4. a) Indus   b) Ganges
    c) Nile   d) Brahmaputra

5. a) Kodaikanal   b) Coonoor
    c) Mussoorie   d) Kochi

6. Which one of the Answer Figure shall complete the given question figure?

Question Figure   Answer Figure

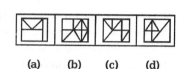

     (a)   (b)   (c)   (d)

7. From the given Answer Figures, select the one in which the Question Figure is hidden/embedded?

Question Figure   Answer Figure

     (a)   (b)   (c)   (d)

8. Which one of the given alternatives would be a meaningful order of the following?

I) Sowing   II) Grain
III) Field   IV) Plouging
V) Harvesting
a) V III IV I II   b) III V II I IV
c) III IV I V II   d) V III IV II I

9. Arrange the following words in the Dictionary order?

1) Arrange   2) Arouse
3) Artillery   4) Aquifer
5) Apron
a) 1 2 3 4 5   b) 2 1 3 4 5
c) 5 4 2 3 1   d) 5 4 2 1 3

Directions (Qns. 10-15): In each of the following questions select the related letters/word/number/Figure from the given alternatives.

10. **Horse : Neighs :: Sheep :?**
a) Yells   b) Chirps
c) Brays   d) Bleats

11. **Calcium : Bone :: Retinol :?**
a) Nerves   b) Eyes
c) Skin   d) Blood

12. **Coconut : Kerala :: Saffron :?**
a) Tamil Nadu   b) Megalaya
c) Jammu & Kashmir   d) Goa

13. **5698 : 9965 :: ? : 8394**
a) 4937   b) 5843
c) 5849   d) 4938

14.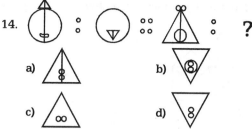

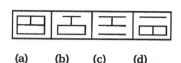

15. **GJM : RVZ : ? : DHL**
a) DIK   b) LNQ
c) EHK   d) CFJ

16. In certain code 'Dog' is coded as '496' 'monkey' is coded as '893210' and 'pig' is coded as '576'. Using this code how will you code the word 'inkpen'?
a) 4 6 8 0 1 6
b) 7 3 2 5 1 3
c) 7 3 5 2 1 3
d) 4 8 6 1 0 8

17. In certain code 'Hai Yei Jai' means 'Good how are'; 'Lai Jai Pai' means 'you are not'. How is 'are' written in that code?
a) Hai   b) lai
c) vai   d) Jai

Direction (Qn. 18): From the given alternative words, select the word which cannot be formed using the letters of the given word.

18. **ADMINISTRATION**
a) RATION   b) STATION
c) ADMIRE   d) TRADITION

Direction (Qn. 19): A word given in capital letters is followed by four answer words. Out of these only one can be formed by using the letters of the given word. Find the word.

19. **IMMEDIATELY**
a) DIAMETER   b) DICTATE
c) DIALECT   d) LIMITED

20. Twenty seven cubes are arranged in a block as shown below. How many will be surrounded by other cubes on all sides?

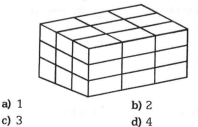

a) 1   b) 2
c) 3   d) 4

21. How many squares are there in the given figure?

   a) 6   b) 8
   c) 10   d) 16

Directions (Qns. 22-23): In a square field four persons A, B, C, D are standing on the four corners as shown below:

Now A & D started walking in clockwise direction, B & C in anti-clockwise direction and occupy the next corners.

22. Who is in the North-East Position?
   a) A   b) B
   c) C   d) D

23. Who is in the South-East Position?
   a) A   b) B
   c) C   d) D

24. Insert the missing number?

$$\begin{array}{cc} 4 & 3 \\ \textcircled{38} & \\ 6 & 5 \end{array} \quad : \quad \begin{array}{cc} 8 & 8 \\ \textcircled{?} & \\ 5 & 6 \end{array}$$

   a) 64   b) 27
   c) 88   d) 96

25. I started walking towards the South for 5 kms and turned towards my sight and walked 6 kms and turned towards East and walked 6 kms. How far I am from the starting point?
   a) 17 kms   b) 5 kms
   c) 12 kms
   d) Returned to the starting point

General English

Directions (Qns. 1-3): There are four words spelt in different ways. Out of them only one is correct. Choose the correct word.

1. a) Circumstances   b) Circumstanses
   c) Circumtances   d) Circamstances

2. a) Nuisence   b) Nusance
   c) Neusense   d) Nuisance

3. a) Greatfullness   b) Greatfulness
   c) Gratefullness   d) Gratefulness

Directions (Qns. 4-8): In these questions, fill in the blanks with an appropriate word.

4. The man died _____ heart attack without getting/receiving any treatment.
   a) off   b) in
   c) by   d) of

5. He went abroad _____ the morning flight.
   a) through   b) on
   c) by   d) off

6. The workers agitated for a fair _____ for their work.
   a) Price   b) Salary
   c) Reward   d) Wage

7. The robbers were arrested and _____ prison yesterday.
   a) taken into   b) taken to
   c) brought to   d) brought in

8. He is too dull _____ this problem.
   a) solving   b) to solving
   c) to solve   d) to do

Directions (Qns. 9-11): In these questions groups of four words each are given. In each group one word is correctly spelt. Find the correctly spelt word.

9. a) Accomodation   b) Accommedation
   c) Accammodation   d) Accommodation

10. a) Skilful   b) Skilfull
   c) Skill fool   d) Skil full

11. a) Hindrence   b) Hinderence
   c) Hindrance   d) Hinderance

Directions (Qns. 12-14): Rearrange the jumbled words.

12. while the/shines/sun/moon/or/make hay.
       A   B   C   D   E   F

13. it is/get/replaced/defective/your booklet/If.
    A   B   C   D   E   F

14. of Spain | he | the Prime Minister
    A   B   C
  has been | as | elected.
     D   E   F

Directions (Qns. 15-18): In each of these questions, a word is given followed by four words marked as A, B, C and D. Find out from the alternatives the word which has OPPOSITE meaning of the word given.

15. **STRANGE**
  a) Unknown   b) Foreign
  c) Astonishing   d) well known

16. **THRUST**
  a) To push forcibly b) To move slowly
  c) To draw close gently
  d) To act quickly

17. **EXHIBIT**
  a) Display   b) Produce
  c) Old one   d) Conceal

18. **LUCENT**
  a) Bright   b) Shining
  c) Dull   d) Light

Directions (Qns. 19-21): In these questions, out of the four alternatives choose the one which can be substituted for the given sentences:

19. **Person who has unusual or remarkable abilities or who is a remarkable example of something.**
  a) Export   b) Genius
  c) Prodigy   d) Scholar

20. **A person who foretells future by reading the palm of one's hand.**
  a) Foreigner
  b) Ophthalmologist
  c) Psychologist
  d) Palmist

21. **One who believes in and fights for equal opportunities for women.**
  a) Womaniser   b) Chauvinist
  c) Effeminate   d) Feminist

Directions (Qns. 22-25): Choose the correct answer.

22. **An adversary is an opponent. Its opposite is _____.**
  a) A companion
  b) An associate
  c) A propanion
  d) An ally

23. **To alleviate something is to lessen it. Its opposite is to _____.**
  a) Exaggerate   b) Incubate
  c) Extricate   d) Aggravate

24. **Authentic means genuine. Its opposite is _____.**
  a) Decrepit   b) Intrepid
  c) Counterfeit   d) Elite

25. **A play is made up of acts. A novel is made up of _____.**
  a) Pages   b) Chapters
  c) Parts   d) Plots

Arithmetic - Numerical Ability

1. **Simplify:**
  $8917 \times 113 + 8917 \times 87 = ?$
  a) 891700   b) 1783400
  c) 169856   d) 1563600

2. **If $A = 4^3 \times 5^2 \times 6$ and $B = 4^2 \times 5 \times 6^2$ then HCF of A and B is**
  a) 168   b) 480
  c) 590   d) 72

3. **Find the value of:**
  $421 \times 0.9 + 130 \times 101$
  a) 13805   b) 13589
  c) 13507   d) 13508.9

4. **What is the value of question mark (?) in the following equation.**
  $4024 + 1632 + 15\%$ of $1496 = ?$
  a) 5890   b) 5884
  c) 5880.4   d) 5888.4

5. **The value of** $\dfrac{(75.8)^2 - (55.8)^2}{20}$ **is**
  a) 125.2   b) 129.6
  c) 131.6   d) 126.5

6. **The value of** $\dfrac{4 - \sqrt{0.04}}{4 + \sqrt{0.4}}$ **is**
  a) 0.904   b) 0.488
  c) 1.23   d) 0.009

7. The least perfect square, which is divisible by each of 21, 36 and 66 is
   a) 213444
   b) 214344
   c) 214434
   d) 231444

8. $\left(\dfrac{1}{2}\right)^{-\frac{1}{2}}$ is equal to
   a) $\dfrac{1}{2}$
   b) $\dfrac{1}{\sqrt{2}}$
   c) $\sqrt{2}$
   d) $2\sqrt{2}$

9. $1 + \dfrac{1}{1 + \dfrac{1}{3}}$ is equal to
   a) $\dfrac{4}{7}$
   b) $\dfrac{7}{4}$
   c) $\dfrac{4}{3}$
   d) $\dfrac{3}{4}$

10. What must be added to make 2203 a perfect square?
    a) 1
    b) 3
    c) 4
    d) 6

11. A cloth merchant on selling 33 metres of cloth obtains a profit equal to the selling price of 11 metres of cloth. Find the profit percentage?
    a) 49
    b) 50
    c) 51
    d) 52

12. In selling an article for Rs. 76, there is a profit of 52%. If it is sold for Rs. 75 then the profit percent will be
    a) 48%
    b) 50%
    c) 54%
    d) Remains the same

13. If the cost price of 10 articles is equal to the selling price of 9 articles, then the gain or loss percent is
    a) $11\dfrac{1}{9}$% profit
    b) $11\dfrac{1}{9}$% loss
    c) $11\dfrac{9}{1}$% loss
    d) $11\dfrac{9}{1}$% profit

14. If the average marks of three batches of 55, 60 and 45 students are respectively 50, 55 and 60, then the average marks of all the students will be
    a) 54.68
    b) 45.86
    c) 64.86
    d) 60

15. The average age of 20 boys in a class is 12 years. 5 new boys are admitted to the class whose average age is 7 years. The average age of the boys in the class becomes _____
    a) 8 years
    b) 9 years
    c) 10 years
    d) 11 years

16. The average of a collection of 20 measurements was calculated to be 56 cm. But later it was found that a mistake had occurred in one of the measurements, which was recorded as 64 cm, but should have been 61 cm. Find the correct average.
    a) 50
    b) 57
    c) 55.85
    d) 59

17. Which number is 40% less than 90?
    a) 36
    b) 50
    c) 60
    d) 54

18. A man *walks* a certain distance and *rides* back in 4 hours 30 minutes. He could *ride* both ways in 3 hours. The time required by the man to *walk* both ways is
    a) 4 hrs 30 mins
    b) 1 hr 30 mins
    c) 5 hrs
    d) 6 hrs

19. The area of a squarefield is 625 sq.km. How long will a horse take to run around it at a speed of 10 km/hr?
    a) 6 hrs
    b) 10 hrs
    c) 8 hrs
    d) 14 hrs

20. The inner circumference of a circular race track 14 m wide is 440 m. Find the radius of the outer circle.
    a) 84 m
    b) 56 m
    c) 70 m
    d) 89 m

21. The sides of a triangle are 5 cm, 12 cm and 13 cm. Find its area.
    a) 30 sq.cm
    b) 15 sq.cm
    c) 29.34 sq.cm
    d) 17.84 sq.cm

22. 25% of water is evaporated from 10 litres of water containing 300 gm of salt. The percentage of salt in the remaining solution is _____
    a) 40%
    b) 30%
    c) 4%
    d) 3%

23. The area of a circular garden is 2464 m². How much distance will have to be covered if you like to cross the garden along its diameter?
    a) 58 m
    b) 56 m
    c) 59 m
    d) 51 m

24. Two pipes can fill a tank separately in 20 minutes and 30 minutes respectively. If both the pipes are opened simultaneously, then the tank will be filled in _____
a) 10 minutes
b) 12 minutes
c) 14 minutes
d) 20 minutes

25. A and B, working separately, can do a piece of work in 10 and 15 days respectively. If they work on alternate days beginning with A, then in how many days will the work be completed?
a) 12 days
b) 13 days
c) 18 days
d) 9 days

TEST No. 14

General Knowledge

1. The nucleus of an atom contains _____
a) Protons and Neutrons
b) Protons and Electrons
c) Protons
d) Electrons and Neutrons

2. Which of the following is ozone depleting pesticide?
a) Benzene
b) D.D.T.
c) Methyl bromide
d) Ethylene

3. When the barometer reading dips suddenly, it is an indication of _____
a) Hot weather
b) Dry weather
c) Storm
d) Calm weather

4. The one who is engaged in scientific drawing of maps is called _____
a) Artist
b) Geographer
c) Geologist
d) Cartographer

5. Good Conductor of electricity is _____
a) dry air
b) glass
c) graphite
d) kerosene

6. Gamma rays are used for _____
a) sterilizing fertilizers
b) cancer therapy
c) treatment of heart disease
d) None of these

7. Fission reaction takes place in _____
a) Hydrogen bomb
b) Atom bomb
c) a reactor as well as in an atom bomb
d) All of these

8. Which soil swells when wet and develops cracks when dry?
a) Alluvial soil
b) Red soil
c) Black soil
d) Laterite soil

9. Most plantations of tea, coffee and fruit are laid out on _____
a) Black soil
b) Delta soil
c) Mountain soil
d) Alluvial soil

10. A landfill is an area where _____
a) garbage is deposited
b) all toxic wastes are buried
c) dead bodies are buried
d) All of the above

11. With the increase in elevation air pressure
a) increases
b) remains the same
c) first increases and then decreases
d) decreases

12. Rhizome is the underground modification of a plant's _____
a) root
b) leaf
c) fruit
d) stem

13. The Rig Veda contains _____
a) rituals to be adopted by people
b) yagnas to be performed
c) history of the Vedic Period
d) hymns in honour of the Gods

14. The partition of Bengal was revoked by the British Government in the year
a) 1919
b) 1917
c) 1905
d) 1911

15. Chandragupta Maurya defeated _____
    a) Alexander   b) Porus
    c) Seleucus   d) None of these

16. The Ain-i-Akbari was written by _____
    a) Firishta   b) Ibn Batuta
    c) Amir Khusro   d) Balban

17. Ramanuja preached _____
    a) Gyan   b) Bhakti
    c) Ahimsa   d) The Vedas

18. Reasonable restrictions on Fundamental Rights can be imposed by _____
    a) Supreme Court   b) Parliament
    c) President   d) None of these

19. The High Court of a State is directly under
    a) President of India
    b) Supreme Court of India
    c) Governor of the State
    d) Chief Justice of India

20. Who among the following has been awarded the Rajiv Gandhi Khel Ratna Award for the year 2008?
    a) Mahendra Singh Dhoni
    b) Harbhajan Singh
    c) Anju Bobby George
    d) Rajyavardhan Singh Rathore

21. Who is the Chief of Naval Staff?
    a) A.P.J. Abdul Kalam b) Suresh Mehta
    c) S. Krishnaswamy   d) N.C. Vij

22. Who is the Governor of Tamil Nadu?
    a) P.S. Rammohan Rao
    b) Surjeet Singh Barnala
    c) T.N. Chaturvedi
    d) M. Rama Jois

23. The 2011 Cricket World Cup will be held in
    a) Australia   b) West Indies
    c) India, Pakistan d) England

24. On which date "Earth Day" is celebrated?
    a) May 23   b) April 23
    c) March 23   d) December 23

25. Which one of the following place is NOT affected by Tsunami that occurred on 26th December 2004?
    a) Dhanushkodi   b) Thiruchendur
    c) Kollam   d) Goa

Reasoning - General Intelligence

1. Which one of the four choice makes the best comparison? REAB is to BEAR as 9832 is to
   a) 2839   b) 2893
   c) 8239   d) 2389

2. Which one of these four is least like the other three?
   a) Bride
   b) Bride groom
   c) Maid
   d) Administrix

3. In certain code "648" means "BOOKS ARE GOOD" and "956" means "I LIKE BOOKS". Using these codes, how will you code the word "BOOKS"?
   a) 6   b) 4
   c) 9   d) 5

Directions (Qns. 4-8): You have to find out the one which is different from the other three responses.

4. a) Running   b) Walking
   c) Standing   d) Climbing

5. a) Low   b) Bark
   c) Bray   d) Bee

6. a) Author   b) Pen
   c) Chisel   d) Anvil

7. a) Eaglet   b) Puppy
   c) Fawn   d) Fish

8. a) Chess   b) Squash
   c) Basket Ball   d) Rugby

Directions (Qns. 9-15): Select one alternative out of (a), (b), (c) & (d) which is analogous to the first.

9. **CHISEL : CARVE :: MATTOCK : ?**
   a) Dig
   b) Amplify
   c) Sow
   d) Cutting

10. **Farmer : Field :: Gambler : ?**
    a) Stage
    b) Casino
    c) Garage
    d) Site

11. **New Zealand : Britain of South :: Holy Land : ?**
    a) India
    b) Rome
    c) Nepal
    d) Palestine

12. **Dove : Peace :: Red Flag : ?**
    a) Revolution
    b) Hospital
    c) Army
    d) Death

13. **19 : 361 :: 24 : ?**
    a) 756
    b) 576
    c) 567
    d) 765

14. **RED : SFE :: BLUE : ?**
    a) ELUD
    b) CEUD
    c) CMFV
    d) CMVF

15. **PLANTS : 6 7 1 5 9 8 :: SLANT : ?**
    a) 5 6 0 4 8
    b) 7 8 2 6 0
    c) 8 7 1 5 9
    d) 3 8 6 1 9

16. **If E = 5, RED = 4, 5, 7 and REED = 21, then DEER = ?**
    a) 42
    b) 12
    c) 23
    d) 21

17. **A word given in capital letters is followed by four answer words. Out of these only one cannot be formed by using the letters of the given word. Find out the word.**

    Question: CONSTRUCTION
    a) COINS
    b) CAUTION
    c) SUCTION
    d) NOTION

18. **From the given alternative words, select the word which can be formed using the letters of the given word.**

    Question: PRAGMATIC
    a) GAME
    b) AGMARK
    c) GUITAR
    d) MAGIC

19. **Arrange the following words in a logical order.**
    I) BUTTERFLY   II) EGG
    III) COCOON   IV) WORM
    a) I III IV II
    b) II I III IV
    c) IV III I II
    d) II IV III I

20. **Which one set of letters when sequentially placed at the gaps in the given letter series shall complete it?**

    Question: t – l – – tta – en – bye by –
    a) lanlee
    b) aeltne
    c) aenlte
    d) aentte

21. **Select the one which is different from the other three responses.**

    A   B   C   D

22. **Select the one which is similar to that of the question figure.**

    Question Figure   Answer Figures

    A   B   C   D

Directions (Qns. 23-25): In the following questions the characters in the first line are the codes for those in the second line and vice-versa. Using these codes, choose the correct code/s for the given word/letters.

λ	θ	A	Y	H	T	I	N	A	Y	I	R	P	ψ	Δ
0	8	4	D	6	M	G	1	4	D	G	7	E	U	B

23. **Using the code "RITA" can be coded as –**
    a) RITA
    b) 7GTA
    c) 7IM4
    d) 7GM4

24. **"θ6ψ0" can be coded as –**
    a) D6ψ8
    b) ψAY6
    c) 8HUλ
    d) 86B4

25. **"1IMHDA" can be coded as –**
    a) 1GHΔ67
    b) NGT6YA
    c) NGTGY4
    d) NGT6Y4

General English

Directions (Qns. 1-5): *In the following passage, some of the words have been left out. Fill in the blanks with the help of the alternatives given.*

Passage: **An organisation *(1)* to two or more persons uniting together to achieve a set of *(2)* goals. When *(3)* work together to realise a common *(4)* they need certain rules and regulations to *(5)* their activities.**

1. a) refers   b) consists
   c) goes   d) helps
2. a) different   b) various
   c) hard   d) common
3. a) factories   b) players
   c) firms   d) people
4. a) goals   b) work
   c) thread   d) practice
5. a) control   b) amend
   c) watch   d) help

Directions (Qns. 6-10): *In each of the following questions, four alternatives are given. You have to choose the nearest 'Antonym' of the given words.*

6. **TACTLESS**
   a) Rude
   b) Careful
   c) Rough
   d) Careless

7. **SOLITARY**
   a) Hidden   b) Retired
   c) Accompanied   d) Lone

8. **HEADLESS**
   a) Attentive   b) Thoughtless
   c) Assertive   d) Head

9. **TRADITIONAL**
   a) Religious   b) Ominous
   c) Modern   d) New

10. **DISGRACE**
    a) Respect
    b) Happy
    c) Loneliness
    d) Disrespect

Directions (Qns. 11-13): *Arrange the following jumbled words into a meaningful sentence.*

11. Physics / Nobel prize for / awarded / was /
        (1)   (2)   (3)   (4)
    C.V. Raman
        (5)
    a) 24351   b) 12543
    c) 54321   d) 54312

12. 16 / Railways is / of zones of / total number /
        (1)   (2)   (3)   (4)
    Indian
        (5)
    a) 43215   b) 43512
    c) 43521   d) 12345

13. Bharatpur / famous / is near / sanctuary /
        (1)   (2)   (3)   (4)
    Ranganthittu.
        (5)
    a) 53214   b) 25431
    c) 13245   d) 24531

Directions (Qns. 14-17): *Each of these questions consists of a word in capital letters, followed by four words or groups of words. Select the word that is most similar in meaning to the word given in capital letters.*

14. **SLOTH**
    a) laziness   b) anger
    c) sludge   d) malady

15. **GLARE**
    a) hatred   b) shine
    c) glassy   d) glide

16. **CRUMPLE**
    a) crying   b) laugh
    c) crush   d) crawl

17. **CONCEAL**
    a) keep secret
    b) covering
    c) sealing
    d) open

Directions (Qns. 18-21): Give one-word substitute from the alternatives for the given expression.

18. **One who is a specialist in treating diseases of the eye.**
    - a) oculist
    - b) optician
    - c) opthalmologist
    - d) none of these

19. **Lasting for a short time**
    - a) Ad hoc
    - b) Fractional
    - c) Transitional
    - d) Ephemeral

20. **Get possession of something again**
    - a) Gain
    - b) Retrieve
    - c) Capture
    - d) Achieve

21. **"Sign" that something good or bad will happen in near future**
    - a) Omen
    - b) Doom
    - c) Forecast
    - d) None of these

Directions (Qns. 22-25): Make your own sentences using the words given below:

22. **VICTIM**

23. **LETHAL**

24. **SATISFACTION**

25. **TO SUFFER**

Arithmetic - Numerical Ability

Directions (Qns. 1-10): Find the value of question mark (?) in each question.

1. **56% of 75 + 9% of 125 = ?**
   - a) 53.25
   - b) 63.25
   - c) 55.25
   - d) 51.25

2. **$\sqrt{?} + 66.4 = 2000 \div 25$**
   - a) 184.96
   - b) 192
   - c) 182.10
   - d) 193

3. **? × 6 = 1920 − 960 = 960**
   - a) 166
   - b) 164
   - c) 162
   - d) 160

4. **$\sqrt{\dfrac{361 \times 324}{19 \times 19}} = ?$**
   - a) 18
   - b) 17
   - c) 324
   - d) 19

5. **$2^{\frac{1}{3}} \times 2^{\frac{1}{2}} \times 3^{\frac{1}{3}} \times 3^{\frac{1}{2}} = ?$**
   - a) 6
   - b) $\dfrac{5}{6_6}$
   - c) $6^{\frac{5}{6}}$
   - d) $6^{\frac{1}{5}}$

6. **10% of 4698 + 134 + 129.6 = ?**
   - a) 49.616
   - b) 4961.6
   - c) 496.16
   - d) 4964.9

7. **$\dfrac{9 - 4.399}{4 + 4.399} \times 100 = ?$**
   - a) 225
   - b) 2.25
   - c) 22.5
   - d) 23.5

8. **$1 + \dfrac{1}{1 + \dfrac{4}{3}} = ?$**
   - a) 14.28
   - b) 1.428
   - c) 142.8
   - d) 14.9

9. **$\dfrac{0.3000}{75} \times 100 \times 9.32 = ?$**
   - a) 374.9
   - b) 3.749
   - c) 37.49
   - d) 3.728

10. **$\sqrt{\dfrac{0.361}{0.00169}} \times \sqrt{\dfrac{361}{1.69}} = ?$**
    - a) 231.45
    - b) 2.314
    - c) 23.45
    - d) 213.45

11. **Find the value of 'x' in the following equation. $\dfrac{2x^2 - 2x - 4x + 4 - 2x - 4}{x^2 - 4}$**
    - a) x = 6
    - b) x = 4
    - c) x = 3
    - d) x = 1

12. **A man swim downstream 12 kmph and upstream 4 kmph; his speed in still water is _____**
    - a) 4 kmph
    - b) 5 kmph
    - c) 7 kmph
    - d) 8 kmph

13. **A train 120 m long takes 30 seconds to cross a platform 330 m long. Calculate the speed of the train in m/sec.**
    - a) 15 m/sec
    - b) 14 m/sec
    - c) 40 m/sec
    - d) 30 m/sec

14. Naresh travels to a place 300 km away at an average speed of 50 kms/hr and returns at 60 kms/hr. Find the approximate average speed of the whole journey.
    a) 54 km/hr
    b) 50 km/hr
    c) 60 km/hr
    d) 42 km/hr

15. A tree 8m in height cast its shadow 5 m long, another tree cast its shadow 25 m long. Find the height of the tree.
    a) 25 m
    b) 30 m
    c) 35 m
    d) 40 m

16. In a Boxing club, the average weight of 45 Boxers is increased by one kg when a Boxer who weighs 55 kg is replaced by a new Boxer. Find the weight of the new boxer.
    a) 50 kg
    b) 75 kg
    c) 85 kg
    d) 100 kg

17. A man rows upstream in 10 minutes and down stream in 15 minutes. Find the velocity of the stream.
    a) 2 kms
    b) 4 kms
    c) 6 kms
    d) 3 kms

18. The sum of money, that will give Re. 1 as Interest per day at the rate of 5% per annum for simple interest is _____
    a) 7350
    b) 7300
    c) 7356
    d) 7200

19. If $7^x = \dfrac{1}{343}$ then the value of x is
    a) $\dfrac{1}{7}$
    b) 3
    c) –3
    d) –7

20. The average of runs scored by a player in 10 innings is 50. How many runs should

he score in the 11th innings, so that his average is increased by 2 runs?
    a) 54
    b) 60
    c) 68
    d) 72

21. The average daily wages of workers of a factory is Rs. 92. There are 300 male and 200 female workers working in the factory. How much money is required for the payment of their salary?
    a) 46,000
    b) 73,600
    c) 92
    d) None of these

22. Each side of a regular hexagon is 1 cm. The area of the hexagon is _____
    a) $3\dfrac{\sqrt{3}}{2}$ cm²
    b) $\dfrac{\sqrt{3}}{2}$ cm²
    c) $\sqrt{3}$ cm²
    d) 1

23. The volume of a perfect circular cylinder is 9πh metre. When h is its height in metres, then the diameter of the base of the cylinder is equal to:
    a) 2 m
    b) 2 m
    c) 6 m
    d) 8 m

24. 25% of the candidates who appeared in an examination failed to qualify and only 450 candidates were qualified. The number of candidates, who appeared in the examination was _____
    a) 500
    b) 370
    c) 575
    d) 600

25. A worker suffers a 10% cut in his wages. He may regain his original wages by obtaining a rise of _____
    a) 10%
    b) 10.10%
    c) 11%
    d) 11.11%

Answers

TEST No. 1

General Knowledge

1. a	2. b	3. d	4. a	5. b	6. c	7. a	8. d	9. d	10. b
11. d	12. c	13. d	14. b	15. d	16. d	17. a	18. c	19. a	20. b
21. b	22. a	23. c	24. b	25. a					

Reasoning - General Intelligence

1. d	2. b	3. b	4. c	5. a	6. a	7. b	8. d	9. b	10. a
11. a	12. c	13. d	14. a	15. d	16. c	17. a	18. a	19. c	20. d
21. b	22. b	23. a	24. d	25. d					

Explanatory Answers

11. The triangles are : ABC, ADC, BCD, ABD, AMD, DMC, BMC, AMB, AEH, BEF, CFG, DGH, AHI, AEI, BEJ, BFJ, CFK, CGK, DGL, DHL

12. The squares are: ABCD, EFGH, EJMI, JMFK, GKML, HLMI

13. The orientation of design is different in figure (4)

14. All other figures can be obtained by rotating any of the figures except figure (1)

15. The letters on adjacent faces of A are B, C, D and F. Therefore, E will be on the face opposite of A.

16. The given number series is based on the following pattern:
$$1 + 5 = 6$$
$$6 + 7 = 13$$
$$13 + 9 = 22$$
$$22 + 11 = 33$$
$$33 + 13 = \boxed{46}$$
$$46 + 15 = 61$$

17. The given number series is based on the following pattern:
$$7 + 5 = 12 \text{ and } 9 + 5 = 14$$
$$12 + 5 = 17 \text{ and } 14 + 5 = \boxed{19}$$

18. The given number series is based on the following pattern:
$$37 - 8 = 29$$
$$29 - 10 = 19$$
$$19 - 2 = \boxed{17}$$
$$17 - 4 = 13$$
$$13 - 6 = 7$$

20.
1	8	9	64	25	216
↓	↓	↓	↓	↓	↓
$(1)^2$	$(2)^3$	$(3)^2$	$(4)^3$	$(5)^2$	$(6)^3$

21. The biggest numbers are 9 and 6.
$9 + 6 = 15$. Smallest number $= 3$
$$15 \div 3 = 5$$
Now, $5 \times 5 = \boxed{25}$

22. C is sister-in-law of B. E is brother of C and also of A. A is the wife of B. Therefore, E is the brother-in-law of B.

23. R > S > P > Q
Clearly, R is the tallest and Q is the smallest.

24. Surendra > Hari > Hameed.....(i)
Hareendra > Harpreet > Hameed ....(ii)
Mahendra > Hareendra ....(iii)
From (i), (ii) and (iii)
Hameed is the youngest.

25. According to question

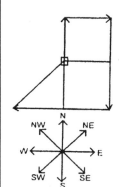

It is clear that hiding place is towards South-West of the place of conversation.

General English

1. d	2. a	3. c	4. c	5. d	6. b	7. c	8. d	9. b	10. b
11. b	12. a	13. c	14. d	15. c	16. b	17. a	18. b	19. d	20. c
21. c	22. b	23. a	24. d	25. a					

Arithmetic - Numerical Ability

1. b	2. b	3. b	4. c	5. b	6. d	7. c	8. b	9. c	10. c
11. b	12. b	13. d	14. d	15. c	16. d	17. a	18. d	19. c	20. c
21. a	22. c	23. c	24. d	25. b					

Explanatory Answers

1. $x \times 11 = 55550 \therefore x = \dfrac{55550}{11} = 5050$

2. $x - 1046 - 398 - 69 = 999; x - 1513 = 999$

   $\therefore x = 999 + 1513 = 2512.$

3. Use the formula: $(a^2 - b^2) = (a + b)(a - b)$

   $1014 \times 986 = (1000 + 14)(1000 - 14) = 1000^2 - 14^2$

   $= 1000000 - 196 = 999804.$

4. $x \times 48 = 173 \times 240;$

   $\therefore x = \dfrac{173 \times 240}{48} = 865$

5. Use the formula: BODMAS {B - bracket, O - of, D - division, M - multiplication, A - addition, S - subtraction}

   $\dfrac{42060}{15} + 5 = 2804 + 5 = 2809.$

7.
   ```
     6.606
      .066
      .66
      .6
   _____
     7.932
   ```

8. $.001 \div x = 0.01$

   $.001 = 0.01 \times x$

   $.1 = \dfrac{.001}{.01} = x$

9. $\dfrac{.24 \times .35}{.14 \times .15 \times .02} = \dfrac{4}{.02} = 200$

10. $\dfrac{1}{3600} = .0002777$

11. $\dfrac{12276}{155} = 79.2$. Now we have put two decimal points in the numerator and one decimal point

in that denominator. Hence, we must get the answer 7.92. But if we put one decimal point in the numerator and two decimal points in the denominator, we will get 792.

13. $(a - b)^2 = a^2 - 2ab + b^2$

    $(9.75 - 5.75)^2 = 9.75^2 - 2 \times 9.75 \times 5.75 + 5.75^2$

    $(4)^2 = 16.$

14. Use the formula: BODMAS {B - bracket, O - of, D - division, M - multiplication, A - addition, S - subtraction}

    $21 \times 1.3 = 27.3 + 3.5 = 30.8$

15. Use the formula: BODMAS {B - bracket, O - of, D - division, M - multiplication, A - addition, S - subtraction}

    $\dfrac{48 - 12 \times 3 + 9}{12 - 9 \div 3} = \dfrac{48 - 36 + 9}{3 + 3} = \dfrac{12 + 9}{6} = \dfrac{21}{6} = 3\dfrac{1}{2}$

16. Use the formula: BODMAS {B - bracket, O - of, D - division, M - multiplication, A - addition, S - subtraction}

    $179 \div 19 \times 9 = 9 \times 9 = 81.$

17. $\dfrac{\sqrt{256}}{\sqrt{x}} = 2; \dfrac{256}{x} = 4; 4x = 256$

    $\therefore x = 64$

18. $\dfrac{112}{\sqrt{196}} \times \dfrac{\sqrt{576}}{12} \times \dfrac{\sqrt{256}}{8} = \dfrac{112}{14} \times \dfrac{24}{12} \times \dfrac{16}{8} = 32$

19. x% of 250 + 25% of 68 = 67

    $\dfrac{x}{100} \times 250 + \dfrac{25}{100} \times 68 = 67$

    $2.5x = 67 - 17 = 50$

    $x = \dfrac{50}{2.5} = 20$

20. $\dfrac{25}{100} \times \dfrac{25}{100} = \dfrac{1}{4} \times \dfrac{1}{4} = \dfrac{1}{16} = .0625$

21. $x - \dfrac{6x}{100} = \dfrac{94x}{100} = .94$ times.

22. $\sqrt{\dfrac{3.6}{100} \times 40} = \sqrt{\dfrac{36 \times 4}{100}} = \dfrac{6 \times 2}{10} = 1.2$

23. A : B = 2 : 3
B : C =   4 : 5
∴ A : B : C = 8 : 12 : 15 $\{\because 2 \times 4; 3 \times 4; 3 \times 5\}$
Now A : C = 8 : 15
     C : D =   6 : 7
∴ A : C : D = 48 : 90 : 105
∴ A : D = 48 : 105 = 16 : 35

24. 24 + (41 × 42) = 24 + 1722 = 1746.

TEST No. 2

General Knowledge

1. c	2. a	3. d	4. b	5. c	6. c	7. d	8. b	9. a	10. c
11. d	12. c	13. d	14. c	15. a	16. a	17. b	18. c	19. a	20. b
21. b	22. a	23. a	24. a	25. c					

Reasoning - General Intelligence

1. c	2. c	3. b	4. c	5. a	6. d	7. d	8. b	9. d	10. c
11. b	12. a	13. b	14. c	15. c	16. a	17. d	18. d	19. c	20. a
21. b	22. a	23. c	24. d	25. c					

Explanatory Answers

1. Both mothers and widows are women.

2. Both writer and teacher are men.

3. Sparrow is a bird, while mouse is different from it.

4. Both tea and coffee are beverages.

5. Some boys and students may be gymnasts.

6. Tank gets doubled filled in 1 minute. Since it gets completely filled in 60 minutes.
   ∴ In 59 minutes, it shall be half-filled.

7. There are clearly 3 ducks which will satisfy the required arrangement.

8. Except (A), all others are prime numbers.

9. Except (D), all others are human properties.

10. Except (C), all others are hill-stations.

11. Except (B), all others are planets.

12. Except (A), all others are mineral elements.

13. 1st term = 1 = 1^2 2nd term = 4 = 2^2
    3rd term = 9 = 3^2 4th term = 25 = 5^2
    5th term = 36 = 6^2
    Hence, ? = 6th term = 7^2 = 49

14. Differences between the consecutive terms of the series are
    5, 10, 15, 20 etc.
    2nd term = 1st term + 5 = 6 + 5 = 11
    3rd term = 2nd term + 10 = 11 + 10 = 21
    4th term = 3rd term + 15 = 21 + 15 = 36
    5th term = 4th term + 20 = 36 + 20 = 56
    Hence, ? = 6th term = 5th term + 25
               = 56 + 25 = 81

15. The rule observed is '× 2 + 1'
    ∴ 2nd term = 1st term × 2+1=3×2+1=7
        3rd term = 2nd term × 2+1=7×2+1=15
        4th term = 3rd term × 2+1=15×2+1=31
        5th term = 4th term × 2+1=31×2+1=63
        Hence, ? = 6th term = 5th term ×2+1
               = 63 × 2 + 1 = 127

16. The differences between the consecutive terms of the series are 2, 6, 6, 10, 10, 14
    ∴ 2nd term = 1st term + 2 = 0 + 2 = 2

3rd term = 2nd term + 6 = 2 + 6 = 8

4th term = 3rd term + 6 = 8 + 6 = 14

5th term = 4th term + 10 = 14+10 = 24

6th term = 5th term + 10 = 24+10 = 34

Hence, ? = 7th term = 6th term + 14

= 34 + 14 = 48.

17. 3rd term = 1st term × 2nd term=19×2=38

5th term = 3rd term × 4th term=38×3=114

Hence, 7th term = 5th term × 6th term

= 114 × 4 = 456

18. Differences between the consecutive terms of the series are 13, 26, 39, 52, etc.

∴ 2nd term = 1st term + 13 = 2 + 13 = 15

3rd term = 2nd term + 26 = 15+26=41

4th term = 3rd term + 39 = 41+39 = 80

5th term = 4th term + 52 = 80+52 = 132

Hence, ? = 6th term = 5th term + 65

= 132 + 65 = 197

19. 2nd term = (1st term)^2 – 1 = 2^2 – 1 = 3

3rd term = (2nd term)^2 – 1 = 3^2 – 1 = 8

4th term = (3rd term)^2 – 1 = 8^2 – 1 = 63

Hence,? = 5th term = (4th term)^2 – 1

= 63^2 – 1 = 3968

20. 2nd term = 1st term ÷5 = 840÷5=168

3rd term = 2nd term ÷ 4 = 168 ÷ 4 = 42

4th term = 3rd term ÷ 3 = 42 ÷ 3 = 14

5th term = 4th term ÷ 2 = 14 ÷ 2 = 7

Hence, ? = 6th term = 5th term ÷ 1

= 7 ÷ 1 = 7

21. As Moon is a satellite, similarly, Earth is a planet.

22. As flower is obtained from a bud, similarly, plant is obtained from a seed.

23. As car is kept in a garage, similarly, aeroplane is kept in a hanger.

24. As chromate is a mineral of chromium, similarly, ilmenite is a mineral of titanium.

25. As radio is manufactured with the help of crystals, similarly, cement is prepared from gypsum.

General English

1. c	2. a	3. b	4. a	5. c	6. a	7. a	8. d	9. d	10. c
11. b	12. c	13. a	14. c	15. b	16. d	17. a	18. c	19. b	20. b
21. b	22. b	23. b	24. b	25. b					

Arithmetic - Numerical Ability

1. a	2. c	3. a	4. a	5. b	6. d	7. c	8. c	9. a	10. c
11. b	12. a	13. a	14. a	15. c	16. b	17. b	18. c	19. a	20. d
21. d	22. a	23. c	24. d	25. b					

Explanatory Answers

1. Increase = 6000 – 4000 = 2000

% of increase = $\dfrac{2000 \times 100}{4000}$ = 50%

2. Increase in strength = 10% of 840

=840× $\dfrac{10}{100}$ = 84

Present total strength = 840 + 84 = 924

3. $\dfrac{130}{150}$ × 100 = 86.6666 ∴ 86.6

4. By using the formula

$\dfrac{a^2 - b^2}{a + b} = \dfrac{(a + b)(a - b)}{(a + b)} = a - b$

Here a = 85, b = 25; a – b = 85 – 25 = 60

5. For (A) the value is 6^2 = 36 ; for (C) it is (8)^2 = 64 for (D) it is 16+4 = 20

But for (B) the value is 4^4 = 256

6. 16 workers can finish the job in 3 hours

1 worker can finish it in 3 ×16 = 48 hours

5 workers can finish it in $\dfrac{48}{5}$ = $9\dfrac{3}{5}$ hours.

7. There are 10 × 9 = 90 different ways to pick 2 socks.

6 × 5 = 30 different ways of picking 2 red socks.

∴ The probability of picking 2 red socks is

$$\frac{6 \times 5}{10 \times 9} = \frac{30}{90} = \frac{1}{3}$$

8. $\frac{1}{2} \times \frac{x}{2} = \frac{x}{4}$

9. $1\frac{1}{4}(x) = \frac{1}{2}; \quad \therefore \quad \frac{5}{4}x = \frac{1}{2};$

$$x = \frac{1}{2} \times \frac{4}{5} = \frac{4}{10} = \frac{2}{5}$$

10. Present age = x – 10

Ten years from now, he will be x – 10 + 10 or x years old.

11. Let the number be x.

From the problem x = 75 + 75% of x

i.e., $x = 75 + \frac{75}{100}x$ i.e., $x = 75 + \frac{3}{4}x$

$$75 = x - \frac{3}{4}x = \frac{1}{4}x \Rightarrow 75 = \frac{1}{4}x$$

∴ x = 300

12. d = 21 cm   ∴ $r = \frac{21}{2}$ cm.

Volume i.e., $\pi r^2 h = 4158$ cm^3

i.e., $4158 = \frac{22}{7} \times \frac{21}{2} \times \frac{21}{2} \times h$

∴ $h = \frac{4158 \times 7 \times 2 \times 2}{22 \times 21 \times 21} = 12$ cm.

Total surface area 2πr (h+r) square units.

$$= 2 \times \frac{22}{7} \times \frac{21}{2}\left(12 + \frac{21}{2}\right) \text{cm}^2$$

$$= 2 \times \frac{22}{7} \times \frac{21}{2} \times \frac{45}{2} \text{cm}^2$$

$$= 11 \times 3 \times 45 = 1485 \text{ cm}^2$$

13. Curved surface area = π r h square units.

$r = \frac{1.4}{2} = 0.7; \; l = 4.2$ cm

∴ curved surface area $= \frac{22}{7} \times 0.7 \times 4.2$

$$= 2.2 \times 4.2 = 9.24 \text{ cm}^2$$

14. Slant height is l

$$l^2 = r^2 + h^2$$
$$= (10.5)^2 + (14)^2$$
$$= 110.25 + 196 = 306.25$$

$l = \sqrt{306.25} = 17.5$ cm.

15. The curved surface area of the cone = πrl square units.

$$= \frac{22}{7} \times 4.9 \times 14 \text{ cm}^2 = 215.6 \text{ cm}^2$$

16. Volume of hemisphere $= \frac{2}{3}\pi r^3$

$$= \frac{2}{3} \times \frac{22}{7} \times 10.5 \times 10.5 \times 10.5 \text{ dm}^3$$

$$= \frac{50935.5}{21} = 2425.5 \text{ dm}^3 = 2425.5 \text{ litres.}$$

17. C.S.A of hemisphere = $2\pi r^2$ square units.

$$= 2 \times \frac{22}{7} \times 1.75 \times 1.75 \text{ cm}^3 = \frac{134.75}{7}$$

$$= 19.25 \text{ cm}^3$$

18. T.S.A of hemisphere = $3\pi r^2$ square units.

$$= 3 \times \frac{22}{7} \times 10 \times 0 \text{ cm}^3 = \frac{6600}{7} = 942.86 \text{ cm}^2$$

19. Surface area of a sphere = $4\pi r^2$ square units.

$$= 4 \times \frac{22}{7} \times 21 \times 21 = 4 \times 22 \times 3 \times 21 = 5544 \text{ cm}^2$$

20. Volume $= \frac{4}{3}\pi r^3$. If the r value is given, volume can be calculated directly and there is no need to apply the total surface area, to find the radius.

Volume $= \frac{4}{3} \times \frac{22}{7} \times 3.5 \times 3.5 \times 3.5$

$$= \frac{539}{3} = 179.67 \text{ cm}^3$$

21. It is known that slant height is l

$l^2 = r^2 + h^2$ ∴ $h^2 = l^2 - r^2; \; h = \sqrt{l^2 - r^2}$

22. $0.00452 = \frac{452}{100000} = \frac{4.52 \times 100}{100000} = 4.52 \times 10^{-3}$

23. When a number is given in scientific notation it is said to be in standard form, i.e., ready for use in logarithmic calculation.

4783 = 4.783 × 1000 = 4.783 × 10^3

24. As per product rule $a^m \times a^n = a^{m+n}$

∴ $x^4 \times x^3 = x^{4+3} = x^7$

25. As per quotient rule $\frac{a^m}{a^n} = a^{m-n}$

here m = 7 and n = 1 ∴ 7 – 1 = 6.

TEST No. 3

General Knowledge

1. c	2. c	3. c	4. a	5. b	6. a	7. c	8. b	9. c	10. c
11. d	12. c	13. a	14. a	15. b	16. b	17. c	18. d	19. a	20. a
21. b	22. b	23. a	24. c	25. a					

Reasoning - General Intelligence

1. a	2. a	3. d	4. b	5. d	6. c	7. b	8. a	9. b	10. d
11. a	12. d	13. a	14. a	15. b	16. d	17. d	18. c	19. d	20. b
21. c	22. d	23. c	24. b	25. a					

Explanatory Answers

5. Here, the series goes like this

   $81 - 12 = 69 - 11 = 58 - 10 = 48 - 9 = 39 - 8 = 31.$

6.
1	2	3	4	5	6	7	8	9
10	11	12	13	14	15	16	17	18

   ↓ 10th position from both ends.

   19

7. See the alternate terms starting from 2nd term in the series: 16, 17, 18, 19, ...

9. The series is $1^2, 2^2, 3^2, 4^2, 5^2, 6^2, 7^2$ ....

   ∴ Missing figure = $6^2 = 36$

10. In the series take alternate terms and see, it is increasing by 5.

    Thus missing figure is $16 + 5 = 21$.

    11, 16, (16+5), ...

19. Square the left hand side. Multiply it by the bottom number. Then divide the result by the right hand number.

22. Except (d), all others are human properties.

23. Except (c), all others are hill-stations.

24. Except (b), all others are planets.

25. Except (a), all others are mineral elements.

General English

1. b	2. a	3. a	4. c	5. d	6. d	7. d	8. c	9. c	10. c
11. b	12. a	13. a	14. b	15. a	16. b	17. a	18. d	19. a	20. c
21. c	22. a	23. d	24. a	25. c					

Arithmetic - Numerical Ability

1. c	2. b	3. d	4. d	5. d	6. a	7. c	8. c	9. a	10. b
11. b	12. a	13. c	14. b	15. c	16. a	17. a	18. c	19. b	20. b
21. b	22. b	23. c	24. d	25. c					

Explanatory Answers

10. Rs. 330 – Rs. 300 = Rs. 30

    i.e. $\dfrac{30}{300} \times 100 = $ Rs. 10

    ∴ $\dfrac{300}{10} \times 100 = $ Rs. 3,000

11. 10 articles for Rs. 8; i.e. 80 paise per article sold for Rs. 1.25; per article bought for = 80 paise

    Gain / article (1.25 – 0.80) = 45 paise

    Gain percent = $\dfrac{45}{80} \times 100 = 56\frac{1}{4}\%$

12. 12½% is $\dfrac{1}{8}$

∴ Selling Price of milk = Rs. 4.80 + Rs. 0.60

= Rs. 5.40

New Rate Selling Price

$\dfrac{16 \text{ (Old Quantity)}}{20 \text{ (New Quantity)}} \times$ Rs. 5.40

$= \dfrac{4}{5} \times 5.40 =$ Rs. 4.32 per litre.

16. River A & River B → Length = 650 miles

Let `X' be the length of River A. River B is 250 less than River A

$$x + x - 250 = 650$$

$$2x = 650 + 250$$

$$x = \dfrac{900}{2} = 450$$

Length of River A = 450 miles

Length of River B = 650–450=200 miles

17. 847 – 770 = 77

770 — 77

100 — 10%

18. Remember a leaf has two pages.

19.

Men	holes	days
20	40	60
10	20	?

$\dfrac{20}{10} \times \dfrac{20}{40} \times 60 = 60$ days.

21. Let the breadth be x; length = 2x;

Area = 2x × x = 2x²

$2x^2 = 4050 \Rightarrow x^2 = 2025$ ∴ x = 45 mtr.

Perimeter = 2(l + b)= 2(2x + x) = 6x = 270

Total cost of fencing = 270 × Rs.2.50

= Rs.675.00

22. A : B : C : 1½ : 3⅓ : 2¾ or $\dfrac{3}{2} : \dfrac{10}{3} : \dfrac{11}{4}$

$\dfrac{18 : 40 : 33}{12}$

A : B : C = 18 : 40 : 33

(sum of the ratio 18 + 40 + 33 = 91)

B's share = $91 \times \dfrac{40}{91}$ = Rs. 40

23. A = 180 – 130 = 50

But A = C (given)

∴ B = 130 – 50 = 80

24. Ignore zeros and reduce to old 4 and new 1 (20,000:5000 = 4 : 1). After 10 days food is available for 20 days for 4 at full ration. For 5 at $\dfrac{1}{2}$ ration, the food will be sufficient for

$\dfrac{4 \times 20 \times 2}{5} = 32$ days.

25. $\dfrac{8 + 4}{5 - 2}$ times 5 : 2 = $\dfrac{12}{3}$ times = 4 times

Length = 4 × 5 = 20 M,

Breadth = 4 × 2 = 8 M.

TEST No. 4

General Knowledge

1. a	2. c	3. a	4. c	5. a	6. b	7. b	8. c	9. c	10. c
11. a	12. d	13. b	14. b	15. b	16. d	17. a	18. a	19. c	20. c
21. a	22. a	23. a	24. c	25. a					

Reasoning - General Intelligence

1. b	2. d	3. b	4. d	5. d	6. c	7. c	8. b	9. c	10. c
11. c	12. c	13. a	14. c	15. d	16. d	17. b	18. b	19. c	20. c
21. d	22. c	23. c	24. c	25. d					

Explanatory Answers

3. See the alternate terms increasing by 7.

13. $\dfrac{514}{2} + 1, \dfrac{258}{2} + 1, \dfrac{130}{2} + 1, \dfrac{66}{2} + 1,$

14. All other numbers are perfect squares.

18. See the alternate terms starting from 2nd term in the series 16, 17, 18, 19, ...

19. A → 1st position → 1
    B → 2nd position → 2 + 1 = 3
    C → 3rd position → 3 + 2 = 5
    D → 4th position → 4 + 3 = 7
    E → 5th position → 5 + 4 = 9
    Hence, 3, 9, 7 stands for B, E, D.

22. (It is an A.P. with common difference 2.9)
    (i.e.) In this series each term is obtained by adding 2.9 to the previous term. Thus the next term should be $(11.1 + 2.9) = 14$.

23. The series goes like this

$$1 \times 0 + 1 = 1$$
$$1 \times 1 + 1 = 2$$
$$2 \times 2 + 1 = 5$$
$$5 \times 3 + 1 = 16$$
$$16 \times 4 + 1 = 65$$

24. The series is generated by adding 2 and 20 alternately. Hence the next term is obtained by adding 20.

    (i.e.) $56 + 20 = 76$.

25. In this series the next term is obtained by interchanging the digits and adding one to the resulting number. Hence the next term is obtained by interchanging digits of 37 and adding one to it.

General English

1. a	2. b	3. a	4. b	5. a	6. c	7. b	8. a	9. d	10. a
11. c	12. c	13. c	14. c	15. C	16. W	17. C	18. C	19. W	20. W
21. b	22. b	23. b	24. a	25. b					

Arithmetic - Numerical Ability

1. b	2. a	3. a	4. a	5. a	6. c	7. a	8. b	9. b	10. d
11. a	12. b	13. a	14. b	15. d	16. d	17. b	18. d	19. d	20. d
21. b	22. b	23. b	24. c	25. b					

Explanatory Answers

1. Suppose one part is = Rs. x
   ∴ Other part = Rs. (1440 – x)
   By hypothesis,

   $$1440 - x = \frac{7}{9}x \text{ or } 12960 - 9x = 7x$$

   or $16x = 12960$ ∴ $x = 810$

   Hence, the smaller part = Rs.(1440 – 810)

   $$= Rs.630$$

2. Suppose C.P. of article = Rs. x Loss = 29 %

   ∴ C.P. of article $= Rs. x \times \dfrac{100 - 29}{100}$

   $$= Rs. x \frac{71}{100}$$

If the article was sold for Rs.84 more,

New S.P. $= Rs. \left(\dfrac{71}{100}x + 84 \right)$

Then, profit % $= \dfrac{\dfrac{71}{100}x + 84 - x}{x} \times 100$

By hypothesis,

$$\frac{8400 - 29x}{100x} \times 100 = 11$$

or $8400 - 29x = 11x$ or $40x = 8400$

or $x = Rs.210$

3. Clearly ABC is an isosceles triangle.

Since AD must be right bisector of BC

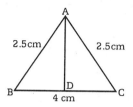

$\therefore$ BD = DC = ½ (4) = 2 cm.

$\therefore$ From right angled D ADB,

$$AB^2 = BD^2 + AD^2$$

or $AD^2 = AB^2 - BD^2 = (2.5)^2 - 2^2 = 6.25 - 4 = 2.25$

$\therefore AD = \sqrt{2.25} = \sqrt{(1.5)^2} = 1.5$ cm.

4. Suppose cost of one table = Rs. x

$\therefore$ Cost of 2 chairs = Rs.x

$\therefore$ Cost of 1 chair = Rs. $\dfrac{x}{2}$

By hypothesis,

$$5\left(\dfrac{x}{2}\right) + 2x = 1350$$

or $5x + 4x = 2700$ or $9x = 2700$;

$\therefore$ x = 300

Hence , total price of one chair and one table

$= Rs.\left(\dfrac{x}{2} + x\right) = Rs.\dfrac{3}{2}x = Rs.\dfrac{3}{2} \times 300 = Rs.450$

5. Average of 6 numbers = 8

$\therefore$ Total of 6 numbers = 6 × 8 = 48. If the required number is x, then

$\dfrac{48 + x}{6 + 1} = 9$ or $48 + x = 63$ or $x = 63 - 48 = 15$

6. The required no. $= \dfrac{7700 \times 1}{275} = 308$

7. The total cost price of 125 shirts = 11250 + 375 = Rs. 11625

$\therefore$ The total selling price of 125 shirts

$= \dfrac{120 \times 11625}{100} = Rs. 13950$

$\therefore$ Selling price of one shirt

$= \dfrac{13950}{125} = Rs. 111.60$

8. The required percentage =

$\dfrac{40}{1200} \times 100 = \dfrac{10}{3} = 3\dfrac{1}{3}$

12. Total age of 33 boys (15.2 × 33) = 501.60

Total age of 30 boys (15.1 × 30) = 453.00

$\overline{ 48.60}$

LESS : New boy's age   16.00

$\overline{ 32.60}$

$\therefore$ Age of one boy $= \dfrac{32.60}{2}$

$= 16.30$

Age of twins 16.3 years

13. Let 'X' be the share given to his son

$x + \dfrac{4x}{7}$ (daughter's share) = 102300

$\dfrac{7x + 4x}{7}$ = 102300

11x   = 102300 × 7

      = 716100

(Son's share) x   = 65100

Wife's share $= \dfrac{6}{7}$ th of share given to his son

$= 65100 \times \dfrac{6}{7}$

= Rs. 55800

14. $\dfrac{60{,}000 - 3{,}600}{100} = 564$

15. $\dfrac{3}{2} + \dfrac{11}{4} + \dfrac{35}{8} = \dfrac{12 + 22 + 35}{8} = \dfrac{69}{8} = 8\dfrac{5}{8}$

16. A – 10% more than B or 15% less than C

B – Rs. 85

A's earning = 85 + 10% of 85 = 93.5

C's earning = $\dfrac{93.5}{85} \times 100 = 110$

17. Let 'B' get 'x'

$\therefore$ A's share is x + 59 .

C's share is x + 59 + 53 = x + 112

x + x + 59 + x + 112 = 600

3x = 600 – 171 = 429

x = 143

$\therefore$ A gets 143 + 59 = 2.02

19. A chair and a table together cost Rs. 100

Let the cost of the table be x

$$(x - 16) + x = \text{Rs. } 100$$
$$2x - 16 = 100$$
$$2x = 100 + 16 = 116$$

(Cost of the table) $x = \dfrac{116}{2} = \text{Rs. } 58$

20. Let the number of 10 paise coins be x

$$x \times 0.10 + 3x \times 0.20 = \text{Rs. } 21$$
$$0.1x + 0.6x = \text{Rs. } 21$$
$$0.7x = \text{Rs. } 21$$

(No. of 10 paise coins) $x = \dfrac{21}{0.7} = 30$

20 paise coins are thrice (the number of 10 paise coins) $30 \times 3 = 90$

No. of 20 paise coins = 90

22. $\dfrac{\text{Original Quantity} + 50\% \text{ of Original Quantity}}{\text{Total Quantity}} \times \text{C.P. per litre}$

$= \dfrac{10 + 50\% \text{ of } 10 \times 4}{10 + 6} = \dfrac{15 \times 4}{16} = \text{Rs. } 3.75$

23. $\dfrac{5(x + 7)}{9} - 3 = 12$

$$\dfrac{5x + 35 - 27}{9} = 12$$
$$5x + 8 = 108$$
$$5x = 100$$
$$x = 20$$

24. $\dfrac{12 \times 15}{12 + 15} = \dfrac{180}{27} = \dfrac{60}{9} = 6\dfrac{2}{3}$ days.

25. $\dfrac{6 \times 10 \times 12}{(6 \times 10) + (10 \times 12) + (12 + 6)}$ multiply by 2

$= \dfrac{720 \times 2}{60 + 120 + 72} = \dfrac{720 \times 2}{252} = 5\dfrac{5}{7}$

∴ A alone can do the work in

$\dfrac{3}{1} \times \dfrac{10 \times 4}{10 - 4} = \dfrac{120}{6} = 20$ days

Of course, B, alone can do the work in

$10 \times \dfrac{3}{1} = 30$ days

TEST No. 5

General Knowledge

1. a	2. b	3. b	4. b	5. c	6. a	7. c	8. a	9. a	10. a
11. c	12. b	13. d	14. b	15. c	16. a	17. a	18. c	19. b	20. a
21. a	22. c	23. b	24. c	25. c					

Reasoning - General Intelligence

1. d	2. a	3. d	4. c	5. b	6. b	7. c	8. a	9. a	10. b
11. a	12. c	13. c	14. a	15. c	16. d	17. c	18. a	19. c	20. c
21. b	22. c	23. a	24. a	25. c					

Explanatory Answers

1. Alternate numbers increase by 6.

2. The series is $1^3, 2^3, 3^3, 4^3, \ldots$

Hence missing figure: $7^3 = 343$

3. In the series take alternate terms and see, it is increasing by 5.

Thus missing figure is $16 + 5 = 21$.

11, 16, (16 + 5), ...

4. By the rule $2 + 3 = 10$; $6 + 5 = 66$;

$7 + 2 = 63$

We see that two numbers are added first and then multiplied by first number. For, example see

$7 + 2 = 9$ then $9 \times 7 = 63$

∴ Here $8 + 4 = 12$; then $8 \times 12 = 96$.

5. As $2 \times 3 = 6$. But here the rule framed as
   $2 \times 3 \rightarrow 6^2 \rightarrow 36$;
   $5 \times 4 \rightarrow 20^2 \rightarrow 40$;
   $3 \times 3 \rightarrow 9^2 \rightarrow 81$;
   $\therefore 5 \times 5 \rightarrow 25^2 \rightarrow 625$

6. From the given expression we see that the multiplicand and the product are interchanged in its place in each case and then divide
   $\therefore 5 \times 40$ must be written as $40 \div 5 = 8$

7. As other numbers are prime

8. Here the rule, $7 + 2 = 59$ comes as;
   $7 + 2 = (7 - 2)(7 + 2) = 59$
   Also $5 + 3 = (5 - 3)(5 + 3) = 28$;
   Thus $5 + 4 = (5 - 4)(5 + 4) = 19$

9. Two successive letters are left in between the given alphabets. Ex: A B C D E F G H I J K L M

10. $(4 \times 6) \div 3 = 8$; $(2 \times 8) \div 4 = 4$;
    $\therefore (6 \times 5) \div 3 = 10$

13. The series goes like this
    $1 \times 0 + 1 = 1$; $1 \times 1 + 1 = 2$;
    $2 \times 2 + 1 = 5$; $5 \times 3 + 1 = 16$;
    $16 \times 4 + 1 = 65$

14. The series goes as
    $1^2 + 3, 2^2 + 3, 3^2 + 3, 4^2 + 3, 5^2 + 3, 6^2 + 3, \ldots$
    Hence the next term is given by $6^2 + 3 = 39$.

19. See the difference between the numbers outside the brackets and multiply the result by 2.

22. $(49 - 19) + 1 = 31$

23. $(280 \div 10 - 20)8 + 6 = (28 - 20) \times 8 + 6 = 8 \times 8 + 6 = 70$
    Here you cannot add $8 + 6$ first. You have to use 'BODMAS' method.

24. Grape is a fruit; others are vegetables.

General English

1. b	2. b	3. c	4. b	5. c	6. b	7. d	8. a	9. c	10. c
11. c	12. c	13. c	14. b	15. b	16. c	17. d	18. W	19. W	20. W
21. W	22. b	23. b	24. G	25. see the notes given below.					

Explanatory Answers

1. 'the' must be introduced before 'best'.
2. 'will come' must be replaced by 'comes'.
3. 'poet' must be replaced by 'poets'.
4. 'too' must be replaced by 'very'.

5. 'man' must be replaced by 'men'.
16. attractive
17. clean
24. He said to me that he would give me a new pen.
25. He said that he had cut his finger.

Arithmetic - Numerical Ability

1. d	2. c	3. b	4. a	5. b	6. c	7. d	8. a	9. b	10. b
11. d	12. c	13. c	14. c	15. b	16. d	17. d	18. a	19. d	20. b
21. d	22. b	23. d	24. d	25. b					

Explanatory Answers

1. L.C.M of 3, 6 and 7 is 42. Multiply each ratio by 42, we get $14 : 7 : 6$
   $\therefore$ First part is $= \dfrac{14}{14 + 7 + 6} \times 81 = \dfrac{14}{27} \times 81 = 42$

2. $\dfrac{4}{\sqrt{0.000625}} = \dfrac{4}{\sqrt{\dfrac{625}{1000000}}}$

$= \dfrac{4}{\dfrac{25}{1000}} = 4 \times \dfrac{1000}{25} = \dfrac{4000}{25} = 160$

3. The product of means is equal to product of extremes.
   $\therefore 6 \times 32 = 24 \times x$; $192 = 24x$;
   $\therefore x = \dfrac{192}{24} = 8$

4. By using the formula

$$\frac{a^2 - b^2}{a + b} = \frac{(a+b)(a-b)}{(a+b)} = a - b$$

Here $a = 85$ $b = 25$ $a - b = 85 - 25 = 60$

5. Let the number be x;

From the problem $x = 75 + 75\%$ of x

i.e., $x = 75 + \frac{75}{100}x;$

i.e., $x = 75 + \frac{3}{4}x$

$75 = x - \frac{3}{4}x = \frac{1}{4}x;$ $75 = \frac{1}{4}x$

$\therefore$ $x = 300$

6. The factors of 24 are 1, 2, 3, 4, 6, 8, 12, 24;
The factors of 30 are 1, 2, 3, 5, 6, 10, 15, 30.

Their common factors are 1, 2, 3, 6;
The greatest is 6. Hence H.C.F. of 24 and 36 is 6.

7. The factors of $\quad$ 6 are 2×3

8 are $2 \times 2 \times 2$

10 are 2×5

L.C.M (least common multiple) is $2^3 \times 3 \times 5 = 120$

8. $\frac{45}{100} \times x + \frac{30}{100} \times 90 = \frac{30}{100} \times 210$

By simplifying, 9 over 20 $\times$ x + 27 = 63;

$\frac{9x + 540}{20} = 63$ or $9x + 540 = 1260$

$9x = 1260 - 540 = 720;$

$x = \frac{720}{9} = 80$

9. Rs. $330 - 300 =$ Rs. 30

i.e., $\frac{30}{300} = 100$ which is 10%;

$\therefore \frac{300}{10} \times 100 = 3000$

10. $C.I. = P\left[\left(1 + \frac{r}{100}\right)^n - 1\right]$

$= 5000\left[\left(1 + \frac{4}{100}\right)\left(1 + \frac{4}{100}\right) - 1\right]$

$= 5000\left[\left(\frac{26}{25}\right)\left(\frac{26}{25}\right) - 1\right]$

$= 5000 \times \frac{676}{625} - 1$

$= 5000 \times \left(1\frac{51}{625} - 1\right) = \frac{5000 \times 51}{625} = 408$

12. Let 'x' be the share of B

$A + B + C$'s share $= 1080$

$(x - 120) + x + (x - 120 + 60) = 1080$

$x - 120 + x + x - 60 = 1080$

$3x - 180 = 1080$

$3x = 1080 + 180$

$x = \frac{1260}{3} = 420$

B's share = Rs. 420

13. $4 \times 10 - 4 \times 8 = 8$. The Aggregate of last four is more and the last number is $8 + 4 = 12$.

14. $\frac{(27)^{n/3} \times (8)^{-n/6}}{(162)^{-n/2}} = \frac{(3^3)^{n/3} \times (2^3)^{-n/6}}{(2 \times 81)^{-n/2}}$

$= \frac{3^n \times 2^{-n/2}}{2^{-n/2} \times (3^4)^{-n/2}} = \frac{3^n}{3^{-2n}} = 3^{n+2n} = 3^{3n}$

Here we used law of indices,

$\left(a^m\right)^n = a^{mn}; \frac{a^m}{a^n} = a^{m-n}; a^m \times a^n = a^{m+n}$

15. If the average height of 10 also was 160 cm, 1600 cm would have been added without any change in the total average.

The fall was a total of $(40 + 10) \times (160 - 156)$ cm = 200 cm

So, the total height of 10 new students = 1600 − 200 = 1400 cm

16. Formula : − $\left[(x - y) = \frac{xy}{100}\right]\%;$

$(25 - 12) - 12\%$ of $25 = 13 - 3 = 10\%$ profit.

17. When Selling Price is the same and percentage of loss on one is equal to the percentage of gain on the other, then overall it is always, loss.

% of Loss $= \frac{12^2}{10^2} = 1.2^2 = 1.44\%$ Loss

18. $900 \times \frac{100 \times 15}{100 + 12\frac{1}{2}} = \frac{900 \times 115 \times 2}{225} =$ Rs. 920

New Selling Price

He has to sell for Rs. 20 more.

19. We may take the speed of boat and speed of current as $(6 + 5) : (6 - 5) = 11 : 1$ which gives speed downstream as $11 + 1 = 12$ KMPH and in 5 Hrs. covers $5 \times 12 = 60$ KM. But the

distance given is only 30 KM. So, the speed of boat is $\dfrac{11}{2} = 5\dfrac{1}{2}$ KMPH. Hence speed of current is $\dfrac{1}{2}$ KMPH. Note the mental process of working.

20. From the problem,

$\dfrac{L}{b} = \dfrac{5}{3}$ Also Lb = 1500; 3L – 5b = 0;

$b = \dfrac{1500}{L}$; $3L - \dfrac{5 \times 1500}{L} = 0$

$3L^2 = 7500$; $L^2 = \dfrac{7500}{3} = 2500 = (50)^2$;

$\therefore$ L = 50

$\therefore$ $b = \dfrac{1500}{50} = 30$

fencing of field (Perimeter) = 2L + 2b = 2(50) + 2(30) = 100 + 60 = 160 mts.

$\therefore$ Cost of fencing = Rs. 160 ($\therefore$ 1m fencing costs Re.1)

21. Difference between 6 × 2½ and 8 × 1½ is 3.

So, the amount is $\dfrac{18}{3}$ × 100 = Rs. 600

22. 2 × 12 + 12% of 12 = 24 + 1.44 = 25.44%

Interest amount = 25 × 25.44 = Rs. 636

23. $8\dfrac{1}{3}$ % means $\dfrac{1}{12}$.

If Capital is Rs. 12, amount = Rs. 13

Instalment amount = $\dfrac{11256 \times 13^3}{12(12^2 + 13^2 + 12 \times 13)}$

$= \dfrac{11256 \times 169 \times 13}{12(144 + 169 + 156)} = \dfrac{11256 \times 169 \times 13}{12 \times 469}$

= 338 × 13 = Rs. 4394

24. Let the cost price be 100;

Marked Price = 10% higher than the cost price

i.e. 100 + $\dfrac{10}{100}$ × 100 = 10

Marked price	=	110
LESS : 10% discount	=	11
Selling price	=	99

Cost price – Selling price = Loss;

100 – 99 = 1

25. In 3600 secs, the distance covered is 54000 mtrs.

$\therefore$ in 15 secs, $\dfrac{15 \times 54000}{3600}$ = 225 mtrs.

Length of the bridge is 150 mtrs.

$\therefore$ length of the train is 225 – 150 = 75 mtrs.

TEST No. 6

General Knowledge

1. a	2. c	3. a	4. c	5. b	6. c	7. a	8. c	9. b	10. c
11. c	12. a	13. b	14. b	15. b	16. a	17. b	18. b	19. c	20. b
21. c	22. c	23. b	24. c	25. a					

Reasoning - General Intelligence

1. b	2. b	3. b	4. c	5. d	6. b	7. c	8. b	9. c	10. c
11. d	12. a	13. d	14. b	15. a	16. d	17. a	18. b	19. d	20. a
21. d	22. b	23. a	24. c	25. b					

Explanatory Answers

1. In this series, the term is obtained by adding previous two terms.

2. See the alternate terms starting from 2nd term in the series 16, 17, 18, 19, ...

3. Here the rule goes like this.

$6 \times 2 = 31 \Rightarrow \dfrac{62}{2} = 31$;

$8 \times 4 = 42 \Rightarrow \dfrac{84}{2} = 42;$

$6 \times 6 = 33 \Rightarrow \dfrac{66}{2} = 33;$

Thus $8 \times 6 = \dfrac{86}{2} = 43$

4. Consider column wise,

Add first two elements and divide by 2 to get third element; so, in third column $7 + 9 = 16$, on dividing by 2, we get the answer as 8.

5. $8+5-3 = 10; 7+6-6 = 7; 14+8-9 = 13.$

6. Here the series goes as

$1^3-1, 2^3-2, 3^3-3, 4^3-4, 5^3-5, 6^3-6, 7^3-7,....$

The next term is $7^3-7 = 343 - 7 = 336.$

7. See the difference between the numbers outside the brackets and multiply by '4'.

10. Here the series goes like,

$1^3 - 1 = 0;$ $4^3 - 4 = 60;$

$2^3 - 2 = 6;$ $5^3 - 5 = 120;$

$3^3 - 3 = 24;$

Hence the next term must be $6^3-6=210.$

11. Here the series goes like,

$2^3 + 3 = 11;$ $3^3 - 3 = 24;$

$4^3 + 3 = 67;$ $5^3 - 3 = 122;$

$6^3 + 3 = 219;$ $7^3 - 3 = 340$

Hence the next term in the series is 340.

12. Let the marks obtained in Mathematics be x and that of English be y. Therefore $x+y=150.$

But $\dfrac{1}{3} x = \dfrac{1}{2} y.$

Therefore $x = \dfrac{1}{2} y \times \dfrac{3}{1} = \dfrac{3}{2} y$

Apply this value of x in the above equation

$\dfrac{3}{2} y + y = 150, \dfrac{5}{2} y = 150.$

Therefore $y = 150 \times \dfrac{2}{5} = 60.$

13. 1, 2, 3, 4, 5, 6, 7, ... 4, 3, 2, 1

$\qquad\quad \downarrow \qquad\qquad \downarrow$

$\qquad$ Shirish $\quad$ Charu

After interchange

1 2 3 4 5 6 7 8 9 10 11 12 13 14

$\qquad\qquad\qquad\qquad\qquad$ 4 3 2 1

$\qquad\qquad\quad \downarrow \qquad\qquad\qquad \downarrow$

$\qquad\qquad$ Charu $\qquad\qquad$ Shirish

Now "Charu's" position is 10th from the right.

14. All other numbers are prime numbers.

16. $(9 \times 4) - 4 = 32, (15 \times 5) - 5 = 70.$ Hence $(17 \times 3) -3 = 48$

17. $8 \times 3 - 3 = 21, 6 \times 5 - 5 = 25.$ Hence $12 \times 2 - 2 = 22.$

18. $\dfrac{4 \times 6}{8} = 3, \dfrac{2 \times 8}{4} = 4.$

Hence $\dfrac{6 \times 5}{10} = 3.$

19. Among the six 8's preceded by 5 in the sequence, only 4 are not followed by 3.

21. Tank filled by first tap in one hour = 1/2

Tank emptied by 2nd tap in one hour = 1/3

Hence actual tank filled in one hour

$= \dfrac{1}{2} - \dfrac{1}{3} = \dfrac{3-2}{6} = \dfrac{1}{6}$

Or the tank will be filled in 6 hours.

22. C.P. of one pencil = 5 paise

Profit = 20%   S.P. $= 5 \times \dfrac{120}{100} = 6$ paise

23. 16 men can finish the work in 25 days

1 man can finish the work in $25 \times 16 = 400$ days

Or, 20 men can finish the work

in $\dfrac{400}{20} = 20$ days.

24. $\dfrac{200}{20} = 10; \dfrac{10}{100} = \dfrac{1}{10} = 0.1$

25. Between 12 and 30 = 2½ times.

140 is 2½ times greater than 56.

General English

1. b	2. c	3. b	4. c	5. d	6. b	7. d	8. a	9. d	10. c
11. c	12. d	13. b	14. a	15. a	16. d	17. c	18. w	19. c	20. w
21. made for		22. look into		23, 24 & 25. see the notes given below.					

Explanatory Answers

1. 'whom' must be replaced by 'who'.
2. 'myself' must be deleted.
3. 'speaking' must be replaced by 'telling'.
4. 'I' must be replaced by 'me'.
14. alien
15. care

16. praise
17. lenient
23. Her mother told her that beauty does not need any ornament.
24. He told his mother that she was unfit for the job.
25. He asked if he could sit in that place for a few minutes.

Arithmetic – Numerical Ability

1. d	2. c	3. b	4. b	5. a	6. b	7. b	8. c	9. a	10. d
11. a	12. b	13. b	14. c	15. b	16. b	17. c	18. a	19. c	20. c
21. a	22. d	23. a	24. d	25. a					

Explanatory Answers

1. Amount in 2 yrs. = Rs. 1000

   Amount in 5 yrs. = Rs. 4000

   ∴ Interest for 3 years = 4000–1000 = Rs. 3000

   $$R = \frac{100 \times SI}{PT} = \frac{100 \times 30}{1000 \times 3} = 33\frac{1}{3}$$

   $$P = \frac{100 \times SI}{RT} = \frac{100 \times 1000}{\frac{100}{3} \times 2}$$

   $$= \frac{100 \times 1000 \times 3}{100 \times 2} = 1500$$

2. Difference between the compound interest and simple interest for 2 years on a certain sum is

   $$= \frac{Pr^2}{100^2}$$

   Hence $90 = \dfrac{P \times 15 \times 15}{100 \times 100}$;

   $$\therefore P = \frac{90 \times 100 \times 100}{15 \times 15} = Rs.\ 4000$$

3. Speed = distance ÷ time = $\dfrac{100}{10}$ = 10 m/sec

   (one km/hr = $\dfrac{5}{18}$ m/sec.)

   ∴ Speed of the train = $10 \times \dfrac{18}{5}$ = 36 kmph

4. First let us find the Cost Price of 15 pencils

   Let the Cost Price of 15 pencils be Rs.x

   By data 80 : 30 = 100 : x

   $$\therefore x = \frac{100 \times 30}{80} = \frac{75}{2} ;$$

   Selling Price of 15 pencils = $\dfrac{(100 + 30)}{100} \times \dfrac{75}{2}$

   ∴ For Rs. 52, the no. of pencils sold =

   $$52 \times \frac{200 \times 15}{130 \times 75} = 16$$

5. $0.05 = \dfrac{5}{100} = \left(\dfrac{5}{100} \times 100\right)\% = 5\%$

6. x % of $\dfrac{5}{8} = \dfrac{8}{5} \Rightarrow x = \dfrac{8}{5} \times \dfrac{100}{1} \times \dfrac{8}{5} = 256$

7. $\dfrac{x}{3} = (x–20) \ (\Rightarrow) \ x = 3\ (x–20) \ (\Rightarrow)\ 2x = 60$

   $(\Rightarrow)\ x = 30$

8. $\dfrac{3}{4}x = 60 \ (\Rightarrow)\ 60 \times \dfrac{4}{3} = 80$

   Half of the number = $\left(\dfrac{1}{2} \times 80\right) = 40$

9. Let the numbers be x and y. Then $x - y = 11$

and $\frac{1}{3}(x + y) = 7$ (or) $x + y = 21$

Solving $x - y = 11$ and $x + y = 21$,

we get $x = 16$, $y = 5$

10. Let the numbers be 3x, 4x and 5x

Total of these numbers = $(24 \times 3) = 72$

$\therefore 3x + 4x + 5x = 72 \ (\Rightarrow) \ x = 6$

The largest number = $5x = 30$

11. $a : b = 2 : 3$ $b : c = 3 : 4$

    $a : b : c = 2 : 3 : 4$

Also $\dfrac{a}{c} = \dfrac{a}{b} \times \dfrac{b}{c} = \dfrac{2}{3} \times \dfrac{3}{4} = \dfrac{1}{2}$; $a : c = 1 : 2$

12. $A : B = 3 : 4$ $B : C = 4 : 5$ $C : D = 6 : 7$

$\therefore \dfrac{A}{D} = \dfrac{3}{4} \times \dfrac{4}{5} \times \dfrac{6}{7} = \dfrac{18}{35} \Rightarrow A : D = 18 : 35$

13. Let $a = 15$, $b = 16$, $c = 17$

Then $s = \dfrac{1}{2}(a + b + c) = 24$

$\therefore s - a = 9$, $s - b = 8$, $s - c = 7$

$\therefore$ Area $= \sqrt{s(s-a)(s-b)(s-c)}$

$= \sqrt{24 \times 9 \times 8 \times 7} = 109.98 \ cm^2$

14. The given fractions are equivalent to $\dfrac{12}{16}, \dfrac{40}{16},$

$\dfrac{15}{16}$. $\therefore$ H.C.F. $= \dfrac{1}{16}$

18. Average × Number = Total

$\therefore$ 21 years × 22 nos = 462 years   ...(1)

22 years × 23 nos = 506 years   ...(2)

$\therefore$ Teacher's age = (2) − (1) = 506 − 462 = 44 years.

19. $A : B = 2 : 3$ $B : C = 4 : 3$

$A : B : C = 8 : 12 : 9$ $\therefore A : C = 8 : 9$

20. A + B's one day's work $= \dfrac{1}{45} + \dfrac{1}{40} = \dfrac{17}{360}$;

Let A leave after x days

$\therefore$ The work done by both in x days =

$\dfrac{17x}{360} = \dfrac{360 - 17x}{360} = \dfrac{23}{40}$

$\therefore x = 9$ Q B has worked for 23 days.

21. $\sqrt{.09} = 0.3$

22. $? = 250 \times 350 - 170 = 87500 - 170 = 87330$

23. $? = 7\dfrac{1}{2} + 6\dfrac{2}{5} - 3\dfrac{1}{4} = \dfrac{15}{2} + \dfrac{32}{5} - \dfrac{13}{4}$

$= \dfrac{75 + 64}{10} - \dfrac{13}{4} = \dfrac{139}{10} - \dfrac{13}{4}$

$= \dfrac{278 - 65}{20} = \dfrac{213}{20} = 10\dfrac{13}{20}$

24. $? = 5.6 \times 4.5 + 3.4 = 25.2 + 3.4 = 28.6$

25. $? = 40.84 \times 5.5 + 4.5 \times 6.40 = 224.62 + 28.8 = 253.42$

TEST No. 7

General Knowledge

1. d	2. a	3. a	4. a	5. c	6. c	7. b	8. c	9. c	10. a
11. b	12. a	13. a	14. c	15. a	16. b	17. c	18. b	19. b	20. a
21. b	22. a	23. a	24. b	25. a					

Reasoning - General Intelligence

1. d	2. a	3. d	4. b	5. c	6. c	7. d	8. b	9. c	10. c
11. b	12. d	13. c	14. a	15. c	16. c	17. c	18. a	19. b	20. d
21. d	22. a	23. b	24. b	25. d					

Explanatory Answers

1. Now U = 2R   (U - Usha's age   R - Rita's age)

    Three years ago, (U – 3) = 3(R – 3)

    $\therefore$ (2R – 3) = 3(R – 3)   ($\therefore$ U = 2R)

    $\Rightarrow$ R = 6 $\Rightarrow$ U = 2 (6) = 12 years.

2. The series is

    $1^2+1, 2^2+2, 3^2+3, 4^2+4, 5^2+5, 6^2+6,...$

    Hence missing figure: $6^2+6 = 42$

3. HKUJ means FISH

    The word FISH is obtained from the word HKUJ by replacing every alphabet by the second alphabet to the left of each alphabet of the word HKUJ. Applying same rule to UVCD, we can see that

    UVCD means STAB

4. Here the rule is

    $2 = 5 \Rightarrow 2 = 2^2 + 1 = 5$;

    $4 = 18 \Rightarrow 4 = 4^2 + 2 = 18$;

    $6 = 39 \Rightarrow 6 = 6^2 + 3 = 39$

    If the same rule is followed, then

    $10 = 10^2 + 5 = 105$;

6. $24 \times 3 = 72 \div 2 = 36$ and so on.

7. See the difference of alternate numbers.

8. Multiply the numbers and add '2'

12. In this, every term is obtained by adding $\frac{1}{3}$ to the previous term.

    Hence the next term must be $\frac{7}{6}$ (i.e.) $1\frac{1}{6}$

    (i.e. It is an A.P. with common difference $\frac{1}{3}$)

16. Work is reduced half and work force is also reduced half.

18. Venice is not a capital city.

20. U.S.A. is not a Commonwealth country.

22. The first, fifth, tenth, fifteenth and so on and rotates within 26 letters.

23. The series goes as $1^2+0, 2^2+1, 3^2+2$ and so on.

24. The series goes on as follows:

    $2^2+2, 3^2–2, 4^2+2, 5^2–2, 6^2+2$

    Hence answer is $7^2 – 2 = 47$

25. The series goes on as follows:

    $2^2+2, 3^3+3, 4^4+4, 5^5+5$

    Hence answer is $6^6+6 = 46662$

General English

1. a	2. c	3. b	4. b	5. c	6. b	7. c	8. c	9. b	10. a
11. c	12. c	13. c	14. b	15. c	16. C	17. W	18. b	19. b	20. d
21. d	22. a	23. b	24. c	25. a					

Explanatory Answers

1. 'It' must be introduced before 'Being'.

2. 'his' must be replaced by 'one's'.

3. 'the' must be introduced before 'best'.

Arithmetic - Numerical Ability

1. a	2. c	3. d	4. c	5. a	6. a	7. a	8. b	9. a	10. c
11. d	12. a	13. c	14. c	15. d	16. c	17. d	18. d	19. b	20. b
21. a	22. a	23. b	24. d	25. c					

Explanatory Answers

1. The sum of remaining two numbers is equal to 5 times; $6 - 3$ times $4 = 30 - 12 = 18$

   $\therefore$ Average $= 18 \div 2 = 9$

2. An amount of Rs. P becomes 2P in 20 years.

   $\therefore$ Rate of interest $= \dfrac{P \times 100}{P \times 20} = 5\%$

3. Compound interest $= P\left[\left(1 + \dfrac{r}{100}\right)^n - 1\right]$

   C.I. $= 3000 \times \left[\left(1 + \dfrac{10}{100}\right)^3 - 1\right] =$

   $3000 \times \left[\left(\dfrac{11}{10}\right)^3 - 1\right] = 3000 \times \left[\dfrac{1331}{1000} - 1\right]$

   $= 3000 \times \dfrac{331}{1000} =$ Rs. 993

4. If A, B and C work together, the job will be finished in

   $\dfrac{1}{7} + \dfrac{1}{14} + \dfrac{1}{28}$ days $= \dfrac{4+2+1}{28} = \dfrac{7}{28} = \dfrac{1}{4}$

   $= 4$ days

5. Curved surface area $= \pi rh$ square units.

   $r = \dfrac{1.4}{2} = 0.7;\ 1 = 4.2$ cm

   $\therefore$ Curved surface area $= \dfrac{22}{7} \times 0.7 \times 4.2$

   $= 2.2 \times 4.2 = 9.24$ cm^2

6. As per the formula $(a + b)^2 = a^2 + 2ab + b^2$

   $12 \times 12 + 2 \times 12 \times 15 + 15 \times 15$

   $= (12 + 15)^2 = (27)^2 = 729$

7. 1m 50 cm $= 150$ cm   1m 80 cm $= 180$ cm

   $\therefore \dfrac{150}{180} = \dfrac{5}{6}$ which is 5 : 6.

8. $50 = 5^2 \times 2$; $40 = 5 \times 2^3$

   $\therefore$ L.C.M $= 5^2 \times 2^3 = 200$

9. In trigonometry, tan X $= \dfrac{\text{opposite side}}{\text{adjacent side}}$

   tan X $= \dfrac{YZ}{XY}$; Here, tan X $= \dfrac{6}{5}$

10. 1 kg = 1000 gms; $\dfrac{510}{1000} = 0.51$ gms.

11. $\dfrac{7}{8} = 0.875;\ \dfrac{6}{7} = 0.857;\ \dfrac{8}{10} = 0.800$ only

    $\dfrac{8}{9} = 0.889$ is the greatest fraction.

12. $150 + 175 = 325;$ 325 m in 13 sec.

    In one second $\dfrac{325}{13} = 25$ metres.

    To convert into km/hr, multiply by (60×60) and divide by 1000

    $\therefore \dfrac{25}{1000} \times 60 \times 60 = 90$ km per hour.

13. A : B = 2 : 3; B : C = 4 : 5

    $\therefore$ A : B : C = 8 : 12 : 15 $\{\because 2 \times 4; 3 \times 4; 3 \times 5\}$

    Now A : C = 8 : 15; C : D = 6 : 7

    $\therefore$ A : C : D = 48 : 90 : 105

    $\therefore$ A : D = 48 : 105 = 16 : 35

14. 10 m. = 1 deca. m.   56 m. = 5.6 deca m.

15. (1) 2 : 5 (2) 3 : 13 (3) 4 : 9 (4) 100 : 1

16. $\left(\dfrac{5}{6} + \dfrac{11}{16}\right) \div \dfrac{73}{24} = \left(\dfrac{40 + 33}{48}\right) \div \dfrac{73}{24}$

    $= \dfrac{73}{48} \times \dfrac{24}{73} = \dfrac{1}{2}$

17. $1 + \dfrac{1}{1 + \dfrac{1}{1 - \dfrac{1}{6}}} = 1 + \dfrac{1}{1 + \dfrac{1}{\dfrac{5}{6}}} = 1 + \dfrac{1}{1 + \dfrac{6}{5}}$

    $= 1 + \dfrac{1}{\dfrac{11}{5}} = 1 + \dfrac{5}{11} = \dfrac{11 + 5}{11} = \dfrac{16}{11}$

18. $? = 4\dfrac{2}{3} + 3\dfrac{1}{5} + 1\dfrac{1}{2}$

    $= (4 + 3 + 1) + \left(\dfrac{2}{3} + \dfrac{1}{5} + \dfrac{1}{2}\right)$

    $= 8 + \left(\dfrac{20 + 6 + 15}{30}\right) = 8 + \dfrac{41}{30}$

19. The number series is based on the following pattern.

    $14.5 + 1 = 15.5; 15.5 + 2 = 17.5;$

    $17.5 + 3 = 20.5; 20.5 + 4 = 24.5; 24.5 + 5 = 29.5$

    Therefore, the number 20 is wrong and it should be replaced by 20.5

20. 30% of 1860 + 40% of 820 = ?% of 3544

    or $\dfrac{30 \times 1860}{100} + \dfrac{40 \times 820}{100} = \dfrac{? \times 3544}{100}$

    or $30 \times 1860 + 40 \times 820 = ? \times 3544$

    $? = \dfrac{55800 + 32800}{3544} = \dfrac{88600}{3544} = 25$

21. We know that

    $\text{Speed} = \dfrac{\text{Distance}}{\text{Time}}$

    According to the question

    Distance = 140 metres

    Time = 7 seconds

$\therefore \text{Speed} = \dfrac{140}{7} = 20$ m/sec.

$\therefore$ Speed in km per hour $= \dfrac{20 \times 18}{5} = 72$ kmph

22. Required price $= \dfrac{748.80}{4 \times 12} \times 29 = $ Rs. 452.40

    = Rs. 450.00

23. $? = \dfrac{19}{7} \times \dfrac{64}{18} \times \dfrac{21}{38} \times \dfrac{54}{16} = 18$

24. Method I

    $? = 999 + 99 + 9999 = 11097$

25. Let the two numbers be x and y.

    $\therefore$ According to the question, x + y = 37 and

    $x \times y = 330$

    We know that $(x - y)^2 = (x + y)^2 - 4xy$

    or, $(x - y)^2 = (37)^2 - 330 \times 4$

    or, $(x - y)^2 = 1369 - 1320$

    or $(x - y)^2 = 49$

    $\therefore x - y = 7$

TEST No. 8

General Knowledge

1. c	2. a	3. a	4. b	5. c	6. b	7. a	8. b	9. a	10. c
11. c	12. b	13. b	14. a	15. c	16. c	17. b	18. b	19. c	20. b
21. b	22. a	23. c	24. b	25. a					

Reasoning - General Intelligence

1. c	2. d	3. d	4. c	5. d	6. a	7. d	8. a	9. a	10. a
11. b	12. c	13. c	14. a	15. a	16. b	17. c	18. c	19. d	20. b
21. b	22. c	23. d	24. c	25. b					

Explanatory Answers

1. $5 + 1^0 = 6; 5 + 2^1 = 7; 5 + 3^2 = 14; 5 + 4^3 = 69; 5 + 5^4 = \boxed{630}$

2. The given number series is based on the following pattern:

   $1 + 1^2 = 2; 2 + 2^2 = 6; 3 + 3^2 = 12; 4 + 4^2 = 20; 5 + 5^2 = 30; 6 + 6^2 = 42; 7 + 7^2 = \boxed{56}$

3.
A → x	B → –
C → ÷	D → +

   Given expression: 50B 10D 3A 25C 5

   After conversion: ? 50 – 10 + 3 × 25 ÷ 5

   = 50 – 10 + 3 × 5 = 50 – 10 + 15

   = 50 + 15 – 10 = 65 – 10 = 55

4. 78321 4562 $\boxed{546}$ 7 632; $\boxed{546}$ 8 5437 $\boxed{546}$

5. The second term is the working place of the first term.

6. Worker and tool relationship has been shown here.

7.

S	U	N
↓	↓	↓
5	7	9

And,

M	O	R	T	A	L
↓	↓	↓	↓	↓	↓
3	6	4	1	2	0

Therefore,

T	A	T	A	S	U	M	O
↓	↓	↓	↓	↓	↓	↓	↓
1	2	1	2	5	7	3	6

8.

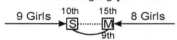

After interchanging positions

Total Number of Girls in the row = 9 + 1 + 5 + 8 = 23 (or) (15 + 9) – 1 = 23

9.

L	A	D	Y
↓	↓	↓	↓
5	1	8	3

And,

P	E	R	S	O	N
↓	↓	↓	↓	↓	↓
9	6	2	7	0	4

Therefore,

P	L	A	Y	E	R
↓	↓	↓	↓	↓	↓
9	5	1	3	6	2

10. It is a domestic bird.

11. All the others have flowing water.

16. Multiply the first number by 3 and reverse the digits,

i.e., $13 \times 3 = 39, 93; 17 \times 3 = 51, 15$

17. $16^2 : 16 - 4 :: 15^2 : 15 - 4$.

18. Take the sum of the numbers outside the triangle and then reverse the digits of the sum so obtained to get the number inside the triangle. Thus,

$15 + 9 + 8 = 32 \Rightarrow 23; 3 + 22 + 4 = 29 \Rightarrow 92$

Similarly, $6 + 7 + 30 = 43 \Rightarrow \boxed{34}$

19. The sum of the first two numbers is equal to the sum of the third and the fourth number in each row. Thus,

$\Rightarrow 15 + 13 = 8 + 20$ or, $28 = 28 \Rightarrow 6 + 3 = 2 + 7$ or, $9 = 9$

Similarly, $\Rightarrow 5 + 9 = ? + 13$ or, $14 = ? + 13$

$\therefore ? = 14 - 13 = 1$

20. The lower left number is twice the lower right number and the upper left number is five times the upper right number.

1st Circle

$9 \times 2 = 18$ and $13 \times 5 = 65$

2nd Circle

$12 \times 2 = 24$ and $17 \times 5 = 85$

3rd Circle

$14 \times 2 = 28$ and $? \times 5 = 55$

$\therefore ? = \dfrac{55}{5} = 11$

21. Second Number = 4 × First Number;

Third Number = 6 × First Number

Thus, $9 \times 4 = 36$ and $9 \times 6 = 54$

Similarly, $12 \times 4 = 48$ and $12 \times 6 = 72$

22. Second Number = (First Number)² + First Number;

Third Number = (First Number)³ – First Number

Thus, $(5)^2 = 25$ and $25 + 5 = 30; (5)^3 = 125$ and $125 - 5 = 120$

Similarly, $(3)^2 = 9$ and $9 + 3 = 12; (3)^3 = 27$ and $27 - 3 = 24$

General English

1.	c	2.	c	3.	c	4.	b	5.	b	6.	b	7.	a	8.	b	9.	a

10. delightful   **11.** attractive   **12.** clean **13.** d   **14.** d   **15.** b   **16.** decision

17. knowledge   **18.** cut off   **19.** to have kept   **20.** bus, would cost

21. us   **22.** whom   **23.** ours   **24. & 25.** see the notes given below.

Explanatory Answers

1. 'but' must be deleted.

2. 'to' must be introduced before 'what'.

3. 'than' must be replaced by 'to'.

24. The teacher said to Chathurvedi that if he did not listen to what he said, he (Chathurvedi) would be punished.

25. The teacher said to the boys that they should complete the exercise before the end of the hour.

Arithmetic - Numerical Ability

1. b	2. d	3. c	4. a	5. c	6. b	7. a	8. b	9. b	10. b
11. a	12. b	13. d	14. c	15. a	16. b	17. b	18. b	19. d	20. b
21. a	22. d	23. a	24. b	25. a					

Explanatory Answers

4. $847 - 770 = 77$; $\dfrac{77}{770} \times 100 = 10\%$

5. $\dfrac{4}{3} \times \dfrac{31}{8} \times \dfrac{5}{8} = \dfrac{155}{48}$

7. A – 10% more than B or 15% less than C;
   B – Rs.85; A's earning $= 85 + 10\%$ of $85 = 93.5$
   C's earning $= \dfrac{93.5}{85} \times 100 = 110$

8. A : B : C : $1\dfrac{1}{2}$: $3\dfrac{1}{3}$: $2\dfrac{3}{4}$ or
   $\dfrac{3}{2}$: $\dfrac{10}{3}$: $\dfrac{11}{4} = \dfrac{18 : 40 : 33}{12}$
   A : B : C = 18 : 40 : 33 (sum of the ratio 18 + 40 + 33 = 91); B's share = $91 \times \dfrac{40}{91}$ = Rs. 40

9. With profit $12\dfrac{1}{2}$ % $\left(\dfrac{1}{8}\right)$, Cost Price is $144 \times \dfrac{8}{9}$ = Rs. 128. Difference of Rs. 16 on each article. Loss on 3 articles broken at Selling Price rate = 3×144 = Rs. 432. Actual loss = Rs. 96. Apparent loss = $432 - 96$ = Rs. 336.
   No. of transistors = $\dfrac{336}{16}$ = 21

11. The ratio of value = $10 \times 7 : 20 \times 4 : 25 \times 3$
    $= 70 : 80 : 75 = 14 : 16 : 15$
    Now the value of $25P = 90 \times \dfrac{15}{45} = 2 \times 15 = 30$ rupees; $\therefore$ No.of 25 P. coins $= 30 \times 4 = 120$.

12. A : B = $\dfrac{1}{5} : \dfrac{1}{4}$; B : C = $\dfrac{1}{2} : \dfrac{1}{3}$
    A : B = 4 : 5; B : C = 3 : 2
    A : B : C = 12 : 15 : 10; Divide in this ratio.

13. Savings should be 20% : 30% or 2 : 3 or 6 : 9
    But they are 3 : 4 or 6 : 8 leftside common
    So, the salaries are in ratio 9 : 8
    That is Rs. $\dfrac{510 \times 9}{17}$ = Rs. 270 = $\dfrac{510 \times 8}{17}$
    = Rs. 240

14. $4 \times 10 - 4 \times 8 = 8$. The aggregate of last four is more and the last number is $8 + 4 = 12$.

15. The value $\sqrt{65^2 - 16^2}$ = 63
    $\because \sqrt{65^2 - 16^2} = \sqrt{(65 + 16)(65 - 16)}$
    $= \sqrt{(81)(49)} = \sqrt{81}\sqrt{49} = 9 \times 7 = 63$

16. From the problem $l = 2b$ (l = length ; b = breadth)
    (Perimeter = $2l + 2b$, if l & b are length & breadth respectively)
    $\therefore$ Perimeter = $2(2b) + 2b = 6b$

17. $\dfrac{5(x+7)}{9} - 3 = 12$; $\dfrac{5x + 35 - 27}{9} = 12$;
    $5x + 8 = 108$; $5x = 100$; $x = 20$

18. From the problem,
    $\dfrac{l}{b} = \dfrac{5}{3}$ Also $lb = 1500$; $3l - 5b = 0$;
    $b = \dfrac{1500}{l}$; $3l - \dfrac{5 \times 1500}{l} = 0$; $3l^2 = 7500$
    $l^2 = \dfrac{7500}{3} = 2500 = (50)^2$
    $\therefore l = 50$ $\therefore b = \dfrac{1500}{50} = 30$
    Fencing of field (Perimeter) = $2l + 2b = 2(50) + 2(30) = 100 + 60 = 160$ mts.
    $\therefore$ Cost of fencing = Rs. 160 ($\because$ 1m fencing costs Re.1)

19. Difference of interest in one year = $(9 \times 8) - (12 \times 3\dfrac{1}{2}) = 72 - 42 = $ Rs. 30
    To cover a difference of $(1200 - 900) = $ Rs. 300
    Time of investment = $\dfrac{300}{30} = 10$ years

20. Distance covered by train to pass the railway signal
    D = 180 m.; Speed V = 90 km/hr

$$= \frac{90 \times 1000}{3600} \text{ m/sec} = 25 \text{ m/sec}$$

$$\text{Required time} = \frac{\text{Distance}}{\text{Speed}} = \frac{180}{25} = 7.2 \text{ sec.}$$

21. $\frac{a}{b} = \frac{1}{3}$; $3a = b$

then $\frac{5a + b}{5a - b} = x$ (let)

$x = \frac{5a + 3b}{5a - 3b} = \frac{8a}{2a} = 4$

22. $0.5 \times A = 0.0003$. $A = \frac{0.0003}{0.5} = 0.0006$

23. Purchasing price of one lemon $= \frac{100}{6}$ paise
    $= 16.66$ paise

Profit $= 20\%$

Selling Price $=$ Purchasing price $+$ profit of one lemon

$$= 16.66 + \frac{16.66 \times 20}{100} = 16.66 + 3.33 = 20 \text{ paise}$$

Therefore, No. of lemons per Rupee $= \frac{100}{20} = 5$

24. $\sqrt{0.0081} = \sqrt{0.09 \times 0.09} = 0.09$

25. $\sqrt{16 + \sqrt{80 + \sqrt{5000 - 4999}}}$

$$= \sqrt{16 + \sqrt{80 + \sqrt{1}}} = \sqrt{16 + \sqrt{81}}$$

$$= \sqrt{16 + 9} = \sqrt{25} = 5$$

TEST No. 9

General Knowledge

1. c	2. a	3. d	4. c	5. b	6. c	7. c	8. a	9. c	10. d
11. a	12. a	13. c	14. a	15. a	16. a	17. a	18. a	19. a	20. a
21. b	22. b	23. d	24. b	25. b					

Reasoning - General Intelligence

1. c	2. b	3. d	4. b	5. b	6. d	7. a	8. a	9. d	10. d
11. d	12. a	13. b	14. a	15. b	16. c	17. c	18. a	19. a	20. b
21. b	22. c	23. c	24. d	25. b					

Explanatory Answers

7. It is square of 30 as 400, 100 and 3600 are squares.

10. Necor Buldon Slock - Danger Rocket Explosion
    Edwan Mynor Necor - Danger Spaceship Fire
    Buldon Gimilzor Gondor - Bad Gas Explosion
    From the above three, we understand
    Buldon - Explosion
    Necor - Danger
    Then 'Slock' must mean 'Rocket'.

12. Ann → Jill
    ↑
    Kelly
    ∴ Kelly is the tallest among the three.

13. Boy - 4 years
    Sister - 4 × 3 = 12 years
    The boy will be 12 years old after '8' years.
    Hence after '8' years, sister's age will be 12 + 8 = 20.

15. Jen caught x frogs
    Lisa caught 4 times as 'Jen' caught
    ∴ Lisa caught 4x
    ∴ Both Lisa & Jen caught 4x + x = 5x
    $\qquad$ 5x = 25; ∴ x = 5
    ∴ Jen caught 5 frogs.

20. Let us take the distance between x and y as 100 km.

Jack takes $\dfrac{100}{30} + \dfrac{100}{10} = \dfrac{100+300}{30}$

$$= \dfrac{400}{30} = 13\dfrac{1}{3} \text{ hrs.}$$

Sandy takes $\dfrac{100}{20} + \dfrac{100}{20} = \dfrac{100+100}{20}$

$$\dfrac{200}{20} = 10 \text{ hrs.}$$

General English

1. d	2. d	3. b	4. b	5. W	6. R	7. W	8. R	9. W	10. W
11. d	12. c	13. d	14. b	15. b	16. c	17. b	18. a	19. a	20. c
21. b	**22, 23, 24** & **25.** see notes given below								

Explanatory Answers

22. My house is opposite to the school.

23. Admission to Standard 'V' is closed.

24. Kharagpur is one of the biggest railway junctions in India.

25. The ancient name of Myanmar is Burma.

Arithmetic - Numerical Ability

1. a	2. c	3. b	4. d	5. d	6. a	7. d	8. d	9. d	10. b
11. c	12. b	13. a	14. d	15. b	16. b	17. d	18. b	19. c	20. d
21. b	22. b	23. b	24. c	25. b					

Explanatory Answers

2. $? = 6\dfrac{1}{4} \div 1\dfrac{2}{3} - 1\dfrac{1}{3}$

$= \dfrac{25}{4} \div \dfrac{5}{3} - \dfrac{4}{3} = \dfrac{25}{4} \times \dfrac{3}{5} - \dfrac{4}{3}$

$= \dfrac{15}{4} - \dfrac{4}{3} = \dfrac{45-16}{12}$

$= \dfrac{29}{12} = 2\dfrac{5}{12}$

8. 40% of 2400 + ? % of 600 = 50% of 3840

or, $\dfrac{40 \times 2400}{100} + \dfrac{? \times 600}{100} = \dfrac{50 \times 3840}{100}$

or, $960 + ? \times 6 = 1920$

or, $? \times 6 = 1920 - 960 = 960$

$\therefore ? = \dfrac{960}{6} = 160$

9. $175 \times ? + 140\%$ of 1200

or $175 \times ? = 140 \times 12$

$\therefore ? = \dfrac{140 \times 12}{175} = 9.6$

16. 10 articles for Rs. 8 i.e. 80 paise per article
sold for Rs. 1.25 per article
Bought for = 80 paise
gain / article = (1.25 − 0.80) = 45 paise
gain percent = $\dfrac{45}{80} \times 100 = 56\dfrac{1}{4}\%$

17. 48% is $\dfrac{216}{25}$ 100% is ?

$\dfrac{100}{48} \times \dfrac{216}{25} = 18$

18. $A : B : C = 1\dfrac{1}{2} : 3\dfrac{1}{3} : 2\dfrac{3}{4}$ or $\dfrac{3}{2} : \dfrac{10}{3} : \dfrac{11}{4}$

$\dfrac{18 : 40 : 33}{12}$

$A : B : C = 18 : 40 : 33$ (sum of the ratio 18 + 40 + 33 = 91)

B's share = $91 \times \dfrac{40}{91}$ = Rs. 40

21. Simple Interest = $\dfrac{P \times r \times t}{100}$

Here, P = 600

r = 18%, t = 9 months = 0.75 year

Simple interest = $\dfrac{600 \times 18 \times 0.75}{100}$ = Rs. 81

22. A : B = 5 : 4 or 10 : 8   .... (1)

B : C = 8 : 35   .... (2)

From equations (1) and (2)

A : C = 10 : 35 = 2 : 7

23. $\sqrt{0.0081} = \sqrt{0.09 \times .009} = 0.09$

24. 8008–8000÷10.00 = x.

x = 8008 – 800 = 7208

25. Average of 9 numbers = 7

Then sum of numbers = 9 × 7 = 63

Average of 7 numbers = 9

Then Sum of numbers = 9 × 7 = 63

Total Sum of 16 numbers = 63 + 63 = 126

Average of 16 numbers = $\dfrac{126}{16}$, $7\dfrac{14}{16}$

TEST No. 10

General Knowledge

1. c	2. b	3. d	4. a	5. a	6. c	7. d	8. c	9. b	10. c
11. a	12. a	13. b	14. b	15. a	16. a	17. c	18. b	19. b	20. b
21. b	22. b	23. c	24. d	25. a					

Reasoning - General Intelligence

1. b	2. c	3. d	4. c	5. a	6. c	7. d	8. d	9. b	10. d
11. c	12. b	13. a	14. c	15. c	16. d	17. d	18. c	19. b	20. a
21. a	22. a	23. c	24. b	25. a					

Explanatory Answers

1. The second term is the capital of the first. Vienna is the capital of Austria. Similarly, Nairobi is the capital of Kenya.

2. The second term is the tool used by the first.

3. The second term is the feminine gender of the first term.

4. All others are kept in library.

5. Except Doctor, all others are related to Art and Culture.

6. Except in the number 3245, in all other numbers the first and the last digits are the same.

7.

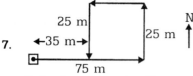

It is clear from the diagram that Raj is 35 metres away from the starting point.

8.

6	5	7

Such combinations are: 6 5 7 , 6 5 7 ;
Thus, there are two such combinations.

9.

10. Name of the city

$\boxed{\text{C}}$ H A N D I G A R $\boxed{\text{H}}$
↓   ↓

1st letter   Last letter

11. Total age of 33 boys and the class teacher = 34 × 14 = 476 years. Total age of 33 boys only = 476 – 47 = 429 years. Average age of boys = $\dfrac{429}{33}$ = 13 years.

12. The given number series is based on the following pattern:

$511 - (13)^2 = 342; 342 + (11)^2 = 463;$

$463 - (9)^2 = 382; 382 + (7)^2 = 431$

$431 - (5)^2 = 406; 406 + (3)^2 = \boxed{415}$

13. The given number series is based on the following pattern:

$7 + 4 = 11; 11 - 3 = 8; 8 + 4 = 12;$

$12 - 3 = 9; 9 + 4 = 13; 13 - 3 = \boxed{10}$

15. In all others, there are two types of figures.

16. In all others, the figure has been divided into two equal parts.

17. From the given figures it is clear that the numbers 1, 6, 5 and 2 cannot be on the face opposite the number 3. Now only the number 4 remains left. Therefore, the number 4 lies opposite 3.

18. L is the daughter of B and D is the brother of L. Therefore, D is the son of B.

A is the brother of B. Therefore, A is the uncle of D.

19. Ram's one day's work $= \dfrac{1}{6}$; Radhika's one day's

work $= \dfrac{1}{12}$

(Ram + Radhika)'s one day's work =

$\dfrac{1}{16} + \dfrac{1}{12} = \dfrac{2+1}{12} = \dfrac{3}{12} = \dfrac{1}{4}$;

Required time = 4 days

20. Since Gokul gave Rs. 100 to Sindhu and Rs. 50 to Komal and Gokul's Rs. 400 were stolen. Therefore, Gokul had $100 + 50 + 400 = 550$

21. Ram → White (does not wear); Arun → Blue (does not wear); Ram → Shyam (different colours); Sunder → Red (wears)

Since there are four persons and only three colours. Therefore, it is not possible to distinguish the colour of all the four. From the above data, it is possible that he wears white. But the data is inadequate.

22. Gopal said this pointing at his son.

23. $\underset{5th}{(1\text{-}4)} \xrightarrow{\hspace{1cm}} \underset{5th}{(6\text{-}9)} \leftarrow$

24. For answering the question, write the alphabets in their proper order and number them from 1 to 26 starting from A and number them in reverse order starting from Z as well.

The number of code letters is the same from Z as the letters of the words have from A.

25. The numbers have a difference of 11, 33, 55, 77 ...... respectively.

General English

1. b	2. d	3. a	4. c	5. c	6. c	7. a	8. c	9. b	10. c
11. c	12. c	13. c	14. b	15. c	16. d	17. d	18. b	19. c	20. b

21, 22, 23, 24 & 25. see notes given below.

Explanatory Answers

1. say : in 'rescuing'
2. No error
3. say : if I 'were' a millionaire
21. antonyms
22. illegible

Present	Past	Past Participle
23. Blow		Blown
24.	Hid	Hidden
25. Wear	Wore	

Arithmetic - Numerical Ability

1. b	2. a	3. a	4. d	5. a	6. d	7. a	8. a	9. b	10. b
11. d	12. b	13. c	14. a	15. c	16. c	17. a	18. c	19. c	20. b
21. d	22. b	23. d	24. b	25. b					

Explanatory Answers

1. Choice a) gives $6^2 = 36$. Choice b) gives $4^4 = 256$. Choice c) is $8^2 = 64$.

   Choice d) is $2 + 4 + 4 = 10$. Choice e) is $4^3 = 64$. Hence (b).

2. The cost of producing the first 8,000 copies is $1,000 + 7,000$ x. Therefore $1,000 + 7,000$ x $= 7,230$ i.e., $7,000$ x $= 6,230$ and therefore x $= 0.89$.

3. $1\dfrac{1}{4}(x) = \dfrac{1}{2}$; $\dfrac{5}{4}x = \dfrac{1}{2}$; x $= \dfrac{2}{5}$

4. Let the number of workers in the institution be x

   The number of workers other than officers = (x – 12)

   The total salary of the 12 officers = Rs.400×12

   ∴ The total salary of the rest = Rs. 56×(x – 12)

   The total salary of all the workers = 60x

   From the problem,

   $60x = (400 \times 12) + 56 \times (x - 12)$;

   i.e. $60x - 56x = 400 \times 12 - 56 \times 12$

   $4x = 12 (400 - 56)$; $4x = (12) (344)$;

   $x = \dfrac{(12 \times 344)}{4}$.

   ∴ Total number of workers = 1032

5. In a km race (i.e. 1,000 m) when A runs 1,000 m, B runs 980 m. Therefore, when A runs 100 m B can run only 98 m. In 500 m race, when B runs 500 m, C runs 485 m.

   When B runs 98 m, C can run $485 \times \dfrac{98}{500}$ m, i.e. 95.06 m

   i.e. when A runs 100 m. B runs 98 m and C runs 95.06 m

   ∴ A beats C by (100 – 95.06). i.e. 4.94 m in a 100 m race.

6. 152 pounds and 4 ounces = 152.25 pounds; $152.25 \div 3 = 50.75$ pounds

   0.75 or 3/4 pounds = 12 ounces.

7. 4 men = 7 boys. i.e. 1 man = $\dfrac{7}{4}$ boys

   ∴ 12 men = $\dfrac{7}{4} \times 12$ boys. i.e. 21 boys

   ∴ 12 men + 8 boys = (21 + 8) boys.

   i.e. 29 boys

   Let x represent the answer required.

No. of boys	No. of days
7	29
29	x

   $\dfrac{7}{29} \times 29 = 7$. ∴ 12 men and 8 boys will take 7 days to do the work.

8. $\left(a + \dfrac{1}{a}\right)^2 = a^2 + \dfrac{1}{a^2} + 2.a.\dfrac{1}{a} = a^2 + \dfrac{1}{a^2} + 2$

   $(5)^2 = a^2 + \dfrac{1}{a^2} + 2$; $25 - 2 = a^2 + \dfrac{1}{a^2}$;

   $23 = a^2 + \dfrac{1}{a^2}$

9. $a^3 + b^3 + c^3 - 3abc = (a + b + c) (a^2 + b^2 + c^2 - ab - bc - ca) = 0$

   (∵ $a + b + c = 0$). ∴ $a^3 + b^3 + c^3 = 3$ abc

10. $\dfrac{40}{1000} = 0.04$

11. By data : 75% of (x + 75) = x.

    i.e. $\dfrac{3}{4}x + 75 = x \Rightarrow 3x + 300 = 4x$

    $\Rightarrow x = 300$

12. A : B : C

    4 : 5

       3 : 8

    12 : 15 : 40

    ∴ A : C = 12 : 40

13. $\dfrac{A}{2} = \dfrac{B}{3} = \dfrac{C}{4} = x$ (say) $\Rightarrow$ A=2x; B=3x; C=4x

    ∴ $2x + 3x + 4x = 8100 \Rightarrow x = 900$

    $\Rightarrow A = 2(900) = 1800$

14. Lowest C.P. is Rs. 200

    Lowest S.P. is Rs. 300 $\Rightarrow$ profit = Rs. 100

    Highest C.P. is Rs. 350

    Highest S.P. is Rs. 425 $\Rightarrow$ profit = Rs. 75

    ∴ Maximum profit = Rs. 100

    Hence, maximum profit on 16 such articles = Rs. (16 × 100) = Rs. 1600.

15. By data : $A = P\left(1 + \dfrac{nr}{100}\right)$

$2{,}442 = P\left(1 + \dfrac{4 \times 12}{100}\right)$

$\Rightarrow P = \dfrac{2{,}442 \times 100}{148} = Rs.\,1{,}650$

16. Let the speed of boat in still water be x km/hr;
Speed of stream be y km/hr

Speed of boat in upstream $= (x - y)$ km/hr;
Speed of boat in downstream $= (x + y)$ km/hr

By hypothesis $\dfrac{9}{x - y} = 3 \Rightarrow x - y = 3$ .....(1)

$\dfrac{18}{x + y} = 3 \Rightarrow x + y = 6$ .....(2)

Adding (1) & (2)

we get $2x = 9 \Rightarrow x = 4.5$ km/hr

17. Common difference between the consecutive terms of the series is 3.

2nd term = 1st term + 3 = 1 + 3 = 4;

3rd term = 2nd term + 3 = 4 + 3 = 7

4th term = 3rd term + 3 = 7 + 3 = 10.
Hence, 5th term = 4th term + 3 = 10 + 3 = 13

18. The required no. $= \dfrac{7700 \times 1}{275} = 308$

19. $? = \dfrac{0.46 - 0.046}{0.046 \div 4.6} = \dfrac{0.414}{0.01} = 41.4$

20. $? = \dfrac{(7.59)^2 - (5.23)^2}{3 - 0.64} = \dfrac{(7.59 + 5.23)(7.59 - 5.23)}{2.36}$

$= \dfrac{12.82 \times 2.36}{2.36} = 12.82$

21. $? = \sqrt{\dfrac{0.361}{0.00169}} ; \sqrt{\dfrac{361}{1.69}} = \sqrt{\dfrac{36100}{169}} = \dfrac{190}{13}$

22. According to question, $\dfrac{1}{10}x = \dfrac{1}{5}y$

$\therefore \dfrac{x}{y} = \dfrac{10}{5} = \dfrac{2}{1}$

$\therefore x : y = 2 : 1$

23. The sum $= \dfrac{n(n+1)}{2} = \dfrac{50(50+1)}{2}$

$= \dfrac{50 \times 51}{2} = \dfrac{2550}{2} = 1275$

$\therefore$ Required average $= \dfrac{1275}{50} = 25.50$

24. The required percentage $= \dfrac{40}{1200} \times 100$

$= \dfrac{10}{3} = 3\dfrac{1}{3}$

25. Let the first and second numbers be x and y respectively.

$\therefore \dfrac{x}{y} = \dfrac{3}{7}$; or, $7x - 3y = 0$ ....(1)

and $\dfrac{x - 12}{y - 12} = \dfrac{9}{37}$; or, $37x - 444 = 9y - 108$

or, $37x - 9y = 336$ ....(2)

By equating above eqn. (1) and (2), we have,
x = 21 and y = 49.

TEST No. 11

General Knowledge

1. d	2. c	3. a	4. a	5. d	6. c	7. c	8. b	9. a	10. a
11. c	12. b	13. d	14. a	15. b	16. d	17. c	18. d	19. d	20. c
21. c	22. d	23. c	24. c	25. b					

Reasoning - General Intelligence

1. a	2. c	3. d	4. c	5. d	6. c	7. a	8. b	9. c	10. a
11. c	12. c	13. d	14. a	15. c	16. a	17. c	18. b	19. c	20. d
21. c	22. a	23. d	24. d	25. c					

Explanatory Answers

1. Except Tomato all others are grown underground

2. $5 \xrightarrow{+2} 7 \xrightarrow{+4} 11 \xrightarrow{+6} 17 \xrightarrow{+8} 25 \xrightarrow{+10} 35$

4. BAROMETERS

MORABSRETE

6.   I   N   D   I   A
      $-3\downarrow$ $-3\downarrow$ $-3\downarrow$ $-3\downarrow$ $-3\downarrow$

       F   K   A   F   X

9. Sculptor is the correct spelling.

10. Pronominal.

11. Mantle

12. Unmindful

14.

15. From the four views of the dice it is clear that the number 1, 3, 4 and 6 cannot be on the face opposite 2.

16.

18. $\left(2^{nd} \text{ row}\right)^2 - \left(1^{st} \text{ row}\right)^2 = 3^{rd}$ row
    i.e. $11 \times 11 - 1 \times 1 = 121 - 1 = 120$;
    $7 \times 7 - 2 \times 2 = 49 - 4 = 45$; $5 \times 5 - 3 \times 3$
    $= 25 - 9 = 16$.

19. $3 + 4 =$ Number below $4 = 7$
    $3 + 4 + 5 =$ Number below $5 = 12$
    $3 + 7 + 12 =$ Number below $12 = 22$
    $3 + 7 =$ Number below $7 = \boxed{10}$

20. The sequences in the given series is
    $+ 3, + 5, + 7, + 9, + 11 ......$

25. ITEM   ACHE
    MITE   EACH

General English

1. c	2. a	3. d	4. a	5. c	6. d	7. b	8. b	9. a	10. c
11. c	12. c	13. a	14. c	15. b	16. a	17. d	18. b	19. b	20. a

7. DECEIVE

8. ADMIRER

9. DEFINITION

10. ANKLE

21. The committe <u>urged</u> the government to train the Law Enforcement personnel.

22. All thieves are <u>knaves</u>.

23. You must <u>impart</u> the truth.

24. She is <u>sobbing</u> on hearing the news.

25. The thief <u>wrested</u> all her jewels.

Arithmetic – Numerical Ability

1. b	2. c	3. b	4. d	5. c	6. d	7. b	8. d	9. c	10. b
11. b	12. b	13. d	14. c	15. d	16. a	17. c	18. b	19. a	20. d
21. c	22. a	23. d	24. a	25. c					

Explanatory Answers

1. $1\dfrac{7}{9} \times \dfrac{9}{20} + 2\dfrac{5}{8} \times 1\dfrac{1}{15}$

$= \left(\dfrac{16}{9} \times \dfrac{9}{20}\right) + \left(\dfrac{21}{8} \times \dfrac{16}{15}\right)$

$= \dfrac{4}{5} + 7 \times \dfrac{2}{5} = \dfrac{18}{5}$

2. $3\dfrac{12}{17} \div 1\dfrac{11}{34} = \dfrac{63}{17} \div \dfrac{45}{34} = \dfrac{63}{17} \times \dfrac{34}{45} = 2\dfrac{4}{5}$

3. $20 \div \left(2 + \overline{5 - 3}\right) = 20 \div (2 + 2) = 20 \times \dfrac{1}{4} = 5$

4. Distance = 72 km; Speed = 60km/hour

Time $= \dfrac{\text{Distance}}{\text{Speed}} = \dfrac{72}{60} = 1.2$

5. D = S × T
Speed = 15 m/s   Time = 4 Hours
Distance = 15 (4 × 60 × 60) = 216000 m
=216 km.

7. $\dfrac{6}{18} \div ? = 18 = \dfrac{6}{18} \times \dfrac{1}{?} = 18 = \dfrac{6}{18 \times 18} = \dfrac{1}{54}$

9. Rotten apples = 25%
Number of Rotten apples = 700

Total number of apples $= \dfrac{700 \times 100}{25} = 2800$

10. $\left(999^2 - 998^2\right) \div 20 \times 100 + 40 = ?$

$= \left[(999 + 998) - (999 - 998)\right] \div 20 \times 100 + 40$

$= \dfrac{1997}{20} \times 100 + 40 = 10025$

11. L.C.M of 3, 6 and 15 = 30.
30 is not between 50 and 100.
∴ 30 × 2 = 60.

12. 32% – 20% = 42 + 30
12% = 72

$\therefore 100\% = \dfrac{12}{100} \times x = 72$

$x = \dfrac{7200}{12} = 600$

100% = 600

13. $v = \dfrac{1}{3}\pi r^2 h = \dfrac{1}{3}\pi \times 6^2 \times 12 = 144\pi$.

14. CP of 12 pens = Rs. 12 (Assumed)
∴ SP of 10 pens = Rs.12

SP of 12 pens $= \dfrac{12}{10} \times 12 = $ Rs.14.40

Gain = Rs. 2.40

Gain % $= \dfrac{2.40}{12} \times 100 = 20\%$

16. Marked price = Rs.300   Discount = 25%

SP $= \dfrac{75}{100} \times 300 = $ Rs.225   Gain = 12.5%

CP $= \dfrac{100}{112.5} \times 225 = $ Rs.200

17. A : B : C = 7 : 8 : 11   LCM = 26

B's Hire charges $= 520 \times \dfrac{8}{26} = $ Rs.160

18. Required difference $= \dfrac{4}{5} \times 700 - \dfrac{5}{7} \times 550$

$= 560 - 393 = 167$

19. Let the two numbers be 5x and 4x.

40% of the first number $= \dfrac{40}{100} \times 5x = 12$

2x = 12
x = 6

50% of the second number $= \dfrac{50}{100} \times 4 \times 6 = 12$

20. $\dfrac{2}{5} \times \dfrac{1}{4} \times \dfrac{3}{7} \times x = 15$

$x = \dfrac{15 \times 5 \times 4 \times 7}{2 \times 3} = 350$

Required number $= \dfrac{1}{2} \times 350 = 175$

21. 1.542 × 2408.69 + 1134.632 = ?

= 3714.1999 + 1134.632

= 4848.19

22. 143% of 3015 + 1974 = 9500 – ?

$= \dfrac{143}{100} \times 3015 + 1974 = 9500 - ?$

= 4311.45 + 1974 = 9500 – ?

= 9500 – 4311.45 – 1974 = 3214.55

24. $16\sqrt{49} + 1492 - 250.52 = ?$

$16 \times 7 + 1492 - 250.52 = ?$

$1604 - 250.52 = 1353.48$

25. $152\sqrt{?} + 795 = 8226 - 3400$

$152\sqrt{?} = 4826 - 795$

$152\sqrt{?} = 4031$

$\sqrt{?} = \dfrac{4031}{152}$

$\sqrt{?} = 26.52$

$? = 703.31$ (approximate value)

TEST No. 12

General Knowledge

1. a	2. c	3. c	4. c	5. d	6. b	7. c	8. a	9. a	10. c
11. b	12. a	13. c	14. d	15. d	16. d	17. a	18. c	19. c	20. b
21. b	22. b	23. d	24. b	25. c					

Reasoning - General Intelligence

1. b	2. b	3. c	4. a	5. d	6. b	7. c	8. b	9. c	10. b
11. d	12. d	13. c	14. b	15. d	16. b	17. d	18. c	19. a	20. d
21. c	22. a	23. d	24. d	25. c					

Explanatory Answers

1. $3 \xrightarrow{+2} G \xrightarrow{+3} D, I \xrightarrow{-2} R \xrightarrow{-3} 7,$

$M \xrightarrow{+2} 6 \xrightarrow{+3} Q$

2. $3 \xrightarrow{+5} D \xrightarrow{+5} J \xrightarrow{+5} Z;$

$G \xrightarrow{+5} 9 \xrightarrow{+5} M \xrightarrow{+5} Q;$

$P \xrightarrow{+5} R \xrightarrow{+5} 6 \xrightarrow{+5} W$

∴ Answer is ZQW

3. 83 is the only prime number.

4. Except 216 others are perfect squares.

5. 'Asteroid' has more than one vowel.

6. Except Lactometer all others are units of measurement.

10. The first 6 letters are written in reverse; the second half is also written in the same way.

11. $40 + 12 \div 3 \times 6 - 60 = 40 + 4 \times 6 - 60$
$= 40 + 24 - 60 = 4$

12. Push × Pull ⇔ throw × pick

14. D R I V E   B E G U M

E I D R V   M G B E U

18. The figures move three steps towards their left; the centre figure rotates 90°.

21. 7, 15, 32, __, 138, 281

$7 \times 2 + 1 = 15, 15 \times 2 + 2 = 32$

$32 \times 2 + 3 = 67$

23.
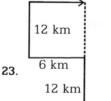

25. A = 4, B = 5, C = 6, D = 7, E = 8, F = 9 .... and so on.

PINK = 19 + 12 + 17 + 14 = 62

RED = 21 + 8 + 7 = 36

General English

1. a	**2.** c	**3.** d	**4.** b	**5.** a	**6.** b	**7.** d	**8.** c	**9.** d	**10.** d
11. a	**12.** b	**13.** a	**14.** d	**15.** c	**16.** will you?		**17.** isn't it?		
18. aren't I?		**19.** c	**20.** c						

Explanatory Answers

19. Raju's father / got / him / a new watch.

       S   + V + IO +   DO

20. Is / he / watching / the TV?

    V+S +   V   +   O

21. Naresh told me that he liked cherry.

22. The police ordered them to leave that place at once.

23. Is she loved by you?

24. She studied well and scored 1180 marks.

25. Very few boys are as clever as Balu.

Arithmetic – Numerical Ability

1. d	**2.** b	**3.** b	**4.** d	**5.** c	**6.** d	**7.** c	**8.** d	**9.** c	**10.** a
11. b	**12.** a	**13.** a	**14.** d	**15.** a	**16.** d	**17.** b	**18.** a	**19.** a	**20.** b
21. c	**22.** a	**23.** a	**24.** c	**25.** c					

Explanatory Answers

1. $x + \dfrac{1}{5} \times \dfrac{1}{3} \times \dfrac{1}{2} = 15 \Rightarrow 450$

2. $x + y = 2(x-y) \Rightarrow x = 3y \Rightarrow x = 3 \times 10 = 30$

3. $10\dfrac{5}{6} \div 91 \Rightarrow \dfrac{65}{6} \div 91 \Rightarrow \dfrac{5}{42}$

4. $\dfrac{1}{2+\dfrac{1}{3+\dfrac{1}{1+\dfrac{1}{4}}}} = \dfrac{1}{2+\dfrac{1}{3+\dfrac{4}{5}}}$

$= \dfrac{1}{2+\dfrac{1}{\dfrac{19}{5}}} = \dfrac{1}{2+\dfrac{5}{19}} = \dfrac{19}{43}$

5. $\dfrac{\sqrt{\left(\sqrt{5}+1\right)^2}}{5-1} = \dfrac{\sqrt{5}+1}{2} = 1.61$

6. $(x + y)^{x/y} = (16)^3 = 4096$

7. $1 : 2 : 3 \Rightarrow x^2 + 2x^2 + 3x^2 = 504$

$14x^2 = 504;\ x^2 = 36;\ x = 6$

Ratio   – $1 : 2 : 3$

The numbers are $6 : 12 : 18$

8. $15 : 5 = 192 : x \Rightarrow x = \dfrac{192 \times 5}{15} = 64$

9. Salary = Rs. 50128 (Annual)

$12\dfrac{1}{2}\% = \dfrac{1}{8}$

$\dfrac{1}{8} \times 50128 = $ Rs. 6266

10. Total age of 30 boys = $14 \times 30 = 420$

When teacher's age is included = $15 \times 31 = 465$

$\therefore 465 - 420 = 45$

11. $1200 \times \left(1 + \dfrac{R}{100}\right)^2 = 1348.32$

$\left(1 + \dfrac{R}{100}\right)^2 = \dfrac{134832}{120000} = \dfrac{11236}{10000} = \left(1 + \dfrac{R}{100}\right)^2$

$= \left(\dfrac{106}{100}\right)^2 = 6\%$

12. Let their ages be $3x : 5x$

$3x + 5x = 80;\ 8x = 80$

$\therefore\ x = 10$

Ratio of their age after 10 years

$= (3x + 10) : (5x + 10) = 40 : 60\ = 2 : 3$

13. Number of failures = 50% of 1100 + 60% of 900

$= \dfrac{50}{100} \times 1100 + \dfrac{60}{100} \times 900 = 1090$

Required Percentage $= \dfrac{1090}{2000} \times 100 = 54.5\%$

14. $\dfrac{392}{\sqrt{x}} = 28 \Rightarrow \sqrt{x} = \dfrac{392}{28} = 14$

15. Required length = HCF of 900, 495 and 1665
= 45 cm

16. Cost price $= 5060 \times \dfrac{100}{110}$ = Rs. 4600

17. $30 \times \dfrac{100}{100 + 50} = 20$ Oranges

18. Interest = Rs. 15767.50 − 8500 = Rs. 7267.50

$\dfrac{7267.50 \times 100}{8500 \times 4.5} = 19$ years

19. Perimeter of Semi circle $= \pi r + d$

$= \dfrac{22}{7} \times \dfrac{63}{2} + 63 = 162$ cm

20. $\dfrac{31}{10} \times \dfrac{3}{10} + \dfrac{7}{5} \div 20 = \dfrac{31 \times 3}{10 \times 10} + \dfrac{7}{5} \times \dfrac{1}{20} = 1$

21. $\dfrac{\sqrt{625}}{11} \times \dfrac{14}{\sqrt{25}} \times \dfrac{11}{\sqrt{196}} = \dfrac{25}{11} \times \dfrac{14}{5} \times \dfrac{11}{14} = 5$

22. $3 \div \left[3 \div \left\{2 \div \dfrac{34}{13}\right\}\right]$

$\Rightarrow 3 \div \left[3 \div \dfrac{26}{34}\right] \Rightarrow 3 \div \dfrac{3 \times 34}{26} \Rightarrow \dfrac{3 \times 26}{3 \times 34} \Rightarrow \dfrac{13}{17}$

23. $\sqrt{7 \times 28} = \sqrt{196} = 14$

24. A alone takes $= \dfrac{1}{36}$ hours; B $= \dfrac{1}{45}$ hours

$\therefore\ A + B = \left(\dfrac{1}{36} + \dfrac{1}{45}\right) = \dfrac{9}{180} = \dfrac{1}{20}$

25. $36 \times \dfrac{5}{18} = 10$ m / sec

Required time $= \dfrac{100}{10} = 10$ sec.

TEST No. 13

General Knowledge

1. b	2. c	3. c	4. b	5. a	6. b	7. b	8. d	9. b	10. d
11. d	12. c	13. a	14. c	15. d	16. a	17. b	18. a	19. d	20. c
21. d	22. b	23. b	24. c	25. d					

Reasoning – General Intelligence

1. c	2. c	3. a	4. c	5. d	6. b	7. b	8. c	9. d	10. d
11. b	12. c	13. a	14. c	15. c	16. b	17. d	18. c	19. d	20. a
21. c	22. a	23. c	24. c	25. b					

Explanatory Answers

1. $45 \xrightarrow{+7} 52 \xrightarrow{+9} 61 \xrightarrow{+11} 72$
$\xrightarrow{+13} 85 \xrightarrow{+15} 100$

2. $4 \xrightarrow{\times 3} 12 \xrightarrow{\times 4} 48 \xrightarrow{\times 5} 240$
$\xrightarrow{\times 6} 1440 \xrightarrow{\times 7} 10080$

3. Except Post Master others are non-living things.

4. Except Nile (River) other three are in India.

5. Kochi is not a hill station.

13. The last number is added one, the remaining numbers are written in reverse order.

15. GJM = G $\xrightarrow{\text{3rd Letter}}$ J $\xrightarrow{\text{3rd Letter}}$ M

EHK = E $\xrightarrow{\text{3rd Letter}}$ H $\xrightarrow{\text{3rd Letter}}$ K

RVZ = R $\xrightarrow{\text{4th Letter}}$ V $\xrightarrow{\text{4th Letter}}$ Z

DHL = D $\xrightarrow{\text{4th Letter}}$ H $\xrightarrow{\text{4th Letter}}$ L

16.
DOG   MONKEY   INK PEN   PIG
↓↓↓   ↓↓↓↓↓↓   ↓↓↓ ↓↓↓   ↓↓↓
496   893210   ::   732   513   576

(22.   & 23)

24.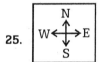
$4 \times 5 = 20$
$6 \times 3 = \underline{18}$
38

25.
Starting Point
6 km | 5 km
·······> East

General English

1. a	2. d	3. d	4. d	5. c	6. d	7. b	8. c	9. d	10. a
11. c	12. FACEDB	13. BECFAD	14. BDFECA	15. d	16. c	17. d
18. c	19. c	20. d	21. d	22. d	23. d	24. c	25. b

Explanatory Answers

12. Make hay/while the/sun/or/moon/shines.
    F   A   C/E   D   B

13. Get/your booklet/replaced/if/it is/defective.
  B   E   C   F/ A   D

14. He/has been/elected/as/the Prime Minister/of Spain.
  B/   D /   F /E/   C   A

Arithmetic - Numerical Ability

1. b	2. b	3. d	4. c	5. c	6. a	7. a	8. c	9. b	10. d
11. b	12. b	13. a	14. a	15. d	16. c	17. d	18. d	19. b	20. a
21. a	22. c	23. b	24. b	25. a

| **Explanatory Answers** |

1. $8917 \times (113 + 87) = 8917 \times 200 = 1783400$

2. Required H.C.F. = product of least power = $4^2 \times 5 \times 6 = 480$

3. $421 \times 0.9 + 130 \times 101 = 378.9 + 13130 = 13508.9$

4. $4024 + 1632 + 1496 \times \dfrac{15}{100} = 5880.4$

5. $\dfrac{(75.8)^2 - (55.8)^2}{20}$

   $= \dfrac{(75.8 + 55.8)(75.8 - 55.8)}{20}$

   $= \dfrac{131.6 \times 20}{20} = 131.6$

6. $\dfrac{4 - \sqrt{0.04}}{4 + \sqrt{0.4}} = \dfrac{4 - 0.2}{4 + 0.2} = \dfrac{3.8}{4.2} = 0.904$

7. $21 = 3 \times 7,\ 36 = 2 \times 2 \times 3 \times 3,$

   $66 = 3 \times 2 \times 11$

   LCM $= 2 \times 2 \times 3 \times 3 \times 7 \times 11$

   Least perfect square divisible by 21, 36, 66 will be $2 \times 2 \times 3 \times 3 \times 7 \times 7 \times 11 \times 11 = 213444$

8. $\left(\dfrac{1}{2}\right)^{-\frac{1}{2}} = \left(2^{-1}\right)^{-\frac{1}{2}} = 2^{\frac{1}{2}} = \sqrt{2}$

9. $1 + \dfrac{1}{1 + \dfrac{1}{3}} = 1 + \dfrac{3}{4} = \dfrac{7}{4}$

10. $\sqrt{2209} = 47$

11. Let the selling price be Re. 1 per metre

    ∴ selling price for 33 metres = Rs. 33

    Profit = Rs. 11

    ∴ Cost price = Rs. 22; selling price = Rs. 33. Profit : 50%

12. Selling price = Rs. 76, profit = 52%

    Cost price $= \dfrac{76 \times 100}{152} = 50$

    If selling price = Rs. 75 then gain = 50%

13. Let the cost price (C.P.) of one article be Re.1

    $\Rightarrow$ C.P. of 10 articles = Rs. 10

Selling price (S.P) of 9 articles = Rs. 10

∴ S.P. of 10 articles = Rs. $\dfrac{100}{9}$

∴ Profit % $= \dfrac{\dfrac{100}{9} - 10}{10} \times 100$

   $= \dfrac{100}{9} = 11\dfrac{1}{9}\%$

14. $\dfrac{55 \times 50 + 60 \times 55 + 45 \times 60}{5 + 60 + 45}$

    $= \dfrac{2750 + 3300 + 2700}{160} = \dfrac{8750}{160} = 54.685$

15. $\dfrac{20 \times 12 + 5 \times 7}{25} = \dfrac{275}{25} = 11$

16. Correct average $= \dfrac{56 \times 20 - 64 + 61}{20} = 55.85$

17. $90 - 40\%$ of $90 = 54$

19. Area is 625 km. ∴ Each side of the field = 25 km

    Perimeter of the field = 100 km. ∴ The horse will take 10 hrs. to run around the field.

20. Inner circumference

    $= 2\pi r = 2 \times \dfrac{22}{7} \times x = \dfrac{44x}{7}$

    $\therefore \dfrac{44x}{7} = 440 \Rightarrow x = 70$

    Radius of the outer circle = 70 + 14 = 84 m

21. The sides of a triangle given are 5, 12 & 13 cm

    $13^2 = 12^2 + 5^2$ (Pythagoras Theorem)

    Area of the $\Delta = \dfrac{1}{2} \times 12 \times 5 = 30$ sq.cm

22. Remaining solution = 7.5 litres contains 300 gm of salt

    $= \dfrac{0.300}{7.5} \times 100 = 4\%$

23. $\pi r^2 = 2464$

    $\Rightarrow r^2 = \dfrac{2464 \times 7}{22} = 784$

    $r = 28, \qquad \therefore D = 56$

24. $\dfrac{1}{20} + \dfrac{1}{30} = \dfrac{1}{12}$ of the tank is filled in one minute.

Time taken by both the pipes to fill the tank

$= \dfrac{20 \times 30}{20 + 30} = \dfrac{600}{50} = 12$ minutes

25. $\dfrac{1}{10} + \dfrac{1}{15} = \dfrac{1}{6}$ of the work is completed in two days.

∴ The whole work will be completed in 12 days.

TEST No. 14

General Knowledge

1. a	2. b	3. c	4. d	5. c	6. b	7. c	8. c	9. c	10. a
11. d	12. d	13. d	14. d	15. c	16. b	17. b	18. b	19. b	20. a
21. d	22. b	23. c	24. b	25. d					

Reasoning - General Intelligence

1. a	2. b	3. a	4. c	5. d	6. a	7. d	8. d	9. a	10. b
11. d	12. a	13. b	14. d	15. c	16. d	17. b	18. d	19. d	20. c
21. d	22. c	23. d	24. c	25. d					

Explanatory Answers

2. Except "Bridegroom" other three denotes the category "Female".

4. Except the word "standing" other three is associated with motion (movements).

5. Low, Bark, Bray are sounds of Animals.

8. Except "Rugby" other three are indoor games.

13. Square of 19, square of 24

14. Next letter in ALPHABETS

15. P = 6, L = 7, A = 1, N = 5, T = 9, S = 8

16. R E E D   7 + 5 + 5 + 4 = 21
    4 + 5 + 5 + 7 = 21 D E E R

General English

1. a	2. d	3. d	4. a	5. a	6. b	7. c	8. a	9. c	10. a
11. c	12. c	13. d	14. a	15. b	16. c	17. a	18. a	19. d	20. b
21. a									

Explanatory Answers

22. The accident victim was taken to the hospital.

23. The mob attacked the shopowners with lethal weapons.

24. Indian consumers have shown their satisfaction with the Korean products.

25. He does not wish to suffer the pain of non-violence.

Arithmetic - Numerical Ability

1. a	2. a	3. d	4. a	5. c	6. c	7. a	8. b	9. d	10. d
11. b	12. d	13. a	14. a	15. d	16. d	17. a	18. b	19. c	20. d
21. a	22. a	23. c	24. d	25. d					

Explanatory Answers

2. $\sqrt{?} + 66.4 = 2000 \div 25$

$\sqrt{?} = 80 - 66.4 = 13.6 = (13.6)^2$

$= \sqrt{184.96}$

3. $? \times 6 = 1920 - 960 = 960$

$? = \dfrac{960}{6} Q = 160$

$? = 160$

5. $2^{\frac{1}{3}} \times 2^{\frac{1}{2}} \times 3^{\frac{1}{3}} \times 3^{\frac{1}{2}} = ?$

$2^{\frac{5}{6}} \times 3^{\frac{5}{6}} = 6^{\frac{5}{6}}$

6. 10% of $4698 + 134 + 129.6$

$= 4961.6 \times \dfrac{10}{100} = 496.16$

8. $1 + \dfrac{1}{1 + \dfrac{4}{3}} = 1 + \dfrac{3}{7}$

$= \dfrac{10}{7} = 1.428$

10. $\sqrt{\dfrac{0.361}{0.00169}} \times \sqrt{\dfrac{361}{1.69}}$

$= \sqrt{213.60} \times \sqrt{213.60}$

$= 14.61 \times 14.61 = 213.45$

11. $\dfrac{2x^2 - 2x - 4x + 4 - 2x - 4}{x^2 - 4} = 0$

$= 2x^2 - 8x = 0$

$= x^2 - 4x = 0$

$= x(x-4) = 0$

$x = 4,\ x = 0$

12. Speed in still water $= \dfrac{1}{2}(12 + 4) = 8$ kmph;

13. $S = \dfrac{D}{T}$

Distance = Length of the train (+) length of the platform

$= 120 + 330 = 450$

Time taken = 30 seconds

∴ m/sec is $450/30 = 15$ m/sec

14. Average speed $= 2xy/x+y$

$= \dfrac{2 + 60 + 70}{60 + 70} = 54.5$ km/hr

15. Height of the tree $= 8 \qquad x$

Shadow length $= 5 \qquad 25$

$= \dfrac{25}{5} \times 8 = 40$ m

16. Increase in Average weight = 1 kg

Increase in total weight $= 45 \times 1 = 45$

∴ The weight of the new boxer is $45 + 55 = 100$ kg

18. $SI = \dfrac{PRT}{100} = 365$

(ie.) Re. 1 per day is Rs. 365 (for a year)

$= \dfrac{365 \times 5 \times 1}{100} = \dfrac{365 \times 100}{5} = $ Rs. 7300

19. $7^x = \dfrac{1}{343} = \dfrac{1}{7^3} = 7^{-3} \Rightarrow x = -3$

20. Let the runs scored in the 11th innings be 'x'.

$= 10 \times 50 + x = 11 \times 52 = 500\ x = 572$

$x = 572 - 500 = 72$ runs

22. Area of a regular hexagon

$= 3\dfrac{\sqrt{3}}{2} \times (\text{side})^2$

$= 3\dfrac{\sqrt{3}}{2} \times 1 = = 3\dfrac{\sqrt{3}}{2}$ cm²

23. $\pi r^2 h = 9\pi h$

$r^2 = 9 \qquad r = 3$ m

Diameter $= 2 \times 3 = 6$ m

24. 25% of the candidates failed

∴ 75% of them have passed

∴ 75% of candidates is = 450

Number of appeared candidates

$= \dfrac{450 \times 100}{75} = 600$

25. $\dfrac{r}{100 - r} \times 100 = \dfrac{10}{100 - 10} \times 100$

$= \dfrac{10}{90} \times 100 = 11.11\%$